Approaching the Benign Environment

Approaching the
Benign Environment

R. BUCKMINSTER FULLER

ERIC A. WALKER

JAMES R. KILLIAN, JR.

PREFACE BY *Taylor Littleton*

COLLIER BOOKS

COLLIER-MACMILLAN LTD., LONDON

Contents

The Contributors

R. BUCKMINSTER FULLER, one of the best known and most admired of contemporary Americans, has a unique record of accomplishment as scientist, philosopher, mathematician, inventor, architectural engineer, and writer.

ERIC A. WALKER, President of Pennsylvania State University, was chief editor of the *Goals Report* of the American Society for Engineering Education, a publication that is exerting a strong influence on the future direction of scientific education in the United States.

JAMES R. KILLIAN, JR., past President and current Chairman of the Corporation of the Massachusetts Institute of Technology, was special assistant for science and technology to President Eisenhower and chairman of the Foreign Intelligence Advisory Board under President Kennedy.

Preface

The Franklin Lectures in the Sciences and Humanities, at Auburn University, are supported by the John and Mary Franklin Foundation of Atlanta, Georgia. They honor the memory of John Leonard Franklin, inventor and philanthropist, in whose life the qualities of humanity, imagination, and self-discipline were combined with a singular technical accomplishment.

To inaugurate the lecture series, the University invited three men whose achievements have long distinguished them as spokesmen for various dimensions of the scientific community—R. Buckminster Fuller, Eric Walker, and James R. Killian—and requested simply that they address themselves, in whatever way they wished, to the general problem of man's retaining his humanity and ideals within a rapidly developing scientific and technological society. All three speakers, each in his own special way, expressed deep concern about the narrow outlook which contemporary education tends to foster in our engineers and scientists, who, paradoxically, are being called upon increasingly as advisors and decision makers to help society resolve many of the social and economic problems which the new technology has created. It is this shared concern, certainly, that underlies Fuller's unique and remarkable historical analysis of the extinction implicit in overspecialization; Walker's conviction that the engineering profession has not properly assumed its social responsibilities; and Killian's advocacy of a new kind of systems approach, originating within universities and involving both scientists and humanists, to aid in the formation of public policy on matters relating to the national well-being.

In addition, however, to this somewhat common point of view, there is in these essays a larger coherent meaning that gives them a special significance. The three scientists are conscious of our failure to cope effectively with the staggering problems that blemish or obscure our national vitality, such as poverty and pollution, transportation, housing, and the tragic failure of the technological marvel of television to enrich and enlarge the mind and spirit of man. They also seem to recognize that our continued development of an alien environment, with all its attendant horror, urgently dictates the forms and directions that our individual and collective efforts must take if we are to define ourselves in the stream of time as a society willing to save itself from its own selfishness and apathy.

Each of these men has been personally involved over many decades in the scientific and technological accomplishments of this country. Each has a long memory and is deeply conscious of America's past and of its connection with the present. Each seems confident of our inherent ability as a nation—with the university as a major center of creativity—to overcome squalor and despair, to halt what Walker describes as a "deterioration in the quality of our lives," and to create, in Killian's phase, a "benign environment." It is indeed this very note of confidence that would seem to align their ideas with those of the students whom they addressed and, to be sure, with those of the great mass of young people today, who desperately wish to see that what each of these men says is eminently possible: a definite connection between education and conscience, between the university and the world.

The ultimate value of these essays, therefore, might well be to advance the hope that the generation currently occupying the seats of national power, with its capacity to mobilize the awesome energy of the country, might respond creatively to the warnings, designs, and the confidence of Americans like Fuller, Walker, and Killian. Indeed, such a national effort could be a genuine answer to concerns often expressed by the rising student generation—the fear that personality cannot triumph over technology, and the suspicion that the nation is unwilling to halt the gradual erosion of our common life. Doubtless, only through this kind of grand but attainable confluence of the power and hopes of the two generations can a benign environment emerge, an environment in which science can be directed toward moral and aesthetic objectives and these enterprises of great pitch and moment do not lose the name of action.

TAYLOR LITTLETON

Auburn, Alabama
September, 1969

Approaching the Benign Environment

Education for Comprehensivity

R. BUCKMINSTER FULLER

I'M VERY GRATEFUL for so cordial an introduction, but I also feel it is necessary when such nice things are said to remind myself that *I* am not impressed, because I know myself too well. I'm quite confident that I have become known at all only because in an age of almost complete specialization I have deliberately set out to be the opposite, to be a comprehensivist; and I have had no competition. If I'd had any, I doubt that I would have come in first. This brings me right away to one of the fine focuses of the Franklin Lectures; that is, to considering the function of higher education and some of the many great changes that may be desirable, and indeed necessary, in our world society within a very short period of time.

I find it surprising that society thinks of specialization as logical, necessary, desirable, if not inevitable. I observe that when nature wants to make a specialist she's very good at it, whereas she seems to have designed man to be a very generally adaptable creature—by far the most adaptable creature we know of. If nature had wanted man to be a specialist, I am sure she would have grown him with one eye and a microscope on it. She has designed no such creatures. I observe that every child demonstrates a comprehensive curiosity. Children are interested in everything and are forever embarrassing their specialized parents by the wholeness of their interests. Children demonstrate right from the beginning that their genes are organized to help them to apprehend, comprehend, coordinate, and employ—in all directions.

Man is not unique in having altered his environment. All living creatures alter the environment in one way or another, and then the altered environment alters them back. There is a chain reaction that goes on, giving rise to what we call evolution. And not only living creatures but every physical system gives off energies entropically, and thereby alters the environment. The universe is a very complex environment altering local processes, but there are creatures that alter their environment in discrete ways, and we find that when they do so, inasmuch as all creatures are processes, the altered environment, in its discrete way, carries out some function of the success of that creature's process.

For instance, a bird alters environment by making a nest, and this is related to its ability to fly. If a bird had to gestate little birds in its womb, it would become so heavy that it would be unable to fly. So we find the bird developing the process of the nest and then issuing forth new life in the form of an egg encasing both the embryo and all the nutriment that is going to be necessary to develop the embryo until it hatches as a chick. There is only one thing to be added: a very discrete amount of heat has to be given to that egg to keep it going along so that the embryo will develop.

In designing that nest, birds demonstrate an interesting adjustment to the delicacy of the process. With a great many migrating birds, the males migrate north earlier than the females and, from their flight advantage, pick areas of the trees where there is going to be the kind of food that that type of bird needs to live—insects or worms or whatever it may be. The males come into the trees and pick positions where nests are going to go. We are familiar with soldiers standing in a tight line and then taking room on the line, spreading out until each man has adequate elbow room. The birds do this in an omni-directional way. Sometimes you see two birds of the same species out on the lawn, and you wonder why they seem to be fighting. What they are doing is taking positions in the trees and then making trial flights to find the nearest insect: they come together, they hit each other, they get interference, and then they spread out in their positions before the time comes to build nests. The males pick domains for their nests and sing their song, and soon the females come along. The female doesn't just stop at the first male she comes to; she waits until she finds the right song and then she comes in. And now they both get busy and build the nest. By the time eggs are laid in the nest, it is a beautiful insulating device; the mother bird sits on top of it, making a total enclosure with high insulation; mother giving off just exactly the right amount of heat to make the egg work. They have situated the nest so that the mother bird is in good position to fly to an insect or a worm, without interference from any other bird, and to get back in time, before the egg goes below the critical heat. All in all, it is an extraordinarily well-balanced design, essential to the successful flight of birds. We have here, then, an externalized function, in that the nest is really part of the womb function. I mention all this in order to make clear that a process, such as the bird, being in several parts which are not integral to one another, can be disassociated from part of its function.

In a sense, my glasses—I'm very farsighted and have been wearing glasses since I was four years old—have become a part of me. I recall being invited in 1930 to speak at Dartmouth College, in what they called Dartmouth Hall. Seventeen years later, in 1947, I was asked to speak at Dartmouth again—and again spoke in Dartmouth Hall. After being introduced as having been there seventeen years before, I stood up and said that while I didn't like to be contradictory, actually I hadn't been there before. My host looked a little surprised, and I pointed out that in the interim Dartmouth Hall had burned down and they had rebuilt it. Moreover, in that seventeen years, all my flesh had completely changed—there was none of the 1930 flesh left. In fact, the only important physical evidence that "I" had been there seventeen years before were my eyeglasses: they were the same ones as before. But nothing else about me was the same. Quite interesting to discover that part of the function "me" was really more permanent than, yet not of, my integral flesh.

Man is not unique, then, as a toolmaker. There are many creatures that make tools, in the way of nests and other apparatus. Man is unique only in the extent to which he has employed tools. All his tools result from the discovery of repeated functions and conditions that are unfriendly or unfavorable to the continuation of the life process. In each case of man's developing or inventing a tool, it is because he has had some experience of need. Man—early man—doesn't have to invent being hungry or thirsty. So he tries out some things, and when he sees that some people die when they eat those red berries, he passes those berries by and keeps looking for something that will keep him going. While looking for his food, he suddenly realizes he is very thirsty and there is no water at hand. In desperation for a while, he finally happens upon some water. Now if you come to water and you are very thirsty and you are just an ancient man, you would have to ask, "How do I take in water?" You might plunge your head under and you get water up your nostrils—that isn't very good. I recall as a child seeing the cat and the dog lapping up their water and wondering if maybe that wasn't a better way. I saw lots of things that animals did which seemed to be very logical. I remember trying to lap water with my tongue, and I found that I couldn't take water in nearly so fast as I could get it if I put in my hand and cupped it, and then I found two hands were even better than one, and I could pour it down like—kloope!

Supposing then that our ancient man has repeated this same process time and again and now has his water—he's still very hungry and must go after berries. And he says, "Everytime I go after berries, I keep losing my water. I wish I could bring this water along with me; yet, if I keep my hands full, this water will probably spill and I can't pick berries." So among the very earliest of all artifacts of man on earth we find vessels or containers of various kinds. From the very beginning, there were men who were able to control environment by taking some of the environment here and moving it to another place so as to have it with them. They were altering the environment in a preferred way to their own advantage.

Once man invents that vessel, several very interesting observations can be made. When he was not using it himself, somebody else could use it. He could make the vessel by scraping out stones, or by scraping out wood, and finally by forming things together—baking clay, weaving baskets, and so forth. Once you develop the vessel, you can also begin to make it of materials that can stand up under heat that your hands couldn't stand. You can make your tool hands much bigger than they had been. You can make them stand acids that your real hands couldn't. In other words, there is a definite basic function for this tool, but you can greatly extend the limits of that functioning—sometimes to such a degree that you don't readily recognize it as an extension of the integral function, as when we get to great tanks and reservoirs. This is something that it is very important to remember about tools.

Thus, man has not been unique in his having developed tools, but he is unique in the extent to which he employs them. And all this comes out of his recognizing repeated experiences and realizing that he can anticipate certain conditions and alter them favorably by making such a thing as a vessel.

As I compare man with other creatures in relation to specialization, I observe that man discovers principles that are operative in his environment and he makes use of those principles. For example, we have the flying bird as a specialist, and the bird does fly beautifully; but when the bird wants to walk, it folds up its wings and therefore has to walk quite awkwardly. The fish swims superbly but can't walk on land. Man can walk on the land, but he also learns the principle of flight, and he puts on his wings and then flies. Then he takes them off so as not to be encumbered by them when he wants to walk again. He can put on his scales and go into the sea, but he is not encumbered by them when he doesn't want to use them. So man has the ability to put on and take off much more than other creatures—which seems to be unique. This is what I mean when I speak about man's general adaptability: the fact that his functions seem to be as little encumbered as possible.

What is really unique is that man is about halfway in the range of size among all creatures—halfway, in the middle of them—and he has extensibility in a great many directions. This, then, says that the specialization should be in the tools and not integral to man himself. The dinosaur had a one-ton tail to knock down bananas when he came to them, but he didn't come to enough bananas to make pulling that one-ton tail around pay off for him. Man invents a ladder that can be left near the trees and out of the way when not in use. And we invent extensible hands and clippers with which to cut things down. We can do all those remote things beautifully.

About eight years ago, two papers were presented at the annual meeting of the American Association for the Advancement of Science, in Philadelphia, one in anthropology and one in biology, that had been written by authors who were unknown to each other. The one in anthropology inquired into the case histories of all the human tribes that have become extinct. The one in biology inquired into the case histories of all the biological species known to become extinct. Both were trying to find a common cause of extinction, and both came up with the same one. Extinction was a consequence of overspecialization.

This is something for us to think about as we begin to go deeper and deeper into our own specialization. How did it happen?

Recalling Darwin's concept of the evolution of species, he speaks about survival only of the fittest. Evolution does not presuppose the elephant stretching his nose and getting bigger and bigger all the while he is alive, altering himself within a generation. Desirable changes occur very gradually from generation to generation. A typical case would be that of a bird that flies over water and lives on certain species of microscopic sea life. Such birds, being able to fly, see that the kinds of sea life they want most tend to get into the marshes along sides of the sea. So we find these birds spending their time in the marshes, enjoying very good hunting for that type of sea life. But then the waters of the earth begin to recede as a consequence of the size of the polar icecaps, and the waters in those marshes become so deep that only birds with long beaks can reach far enough into the water to get at the food they need. The birds with shorter beaks can't get at the food, and they die. This leaves only the long beakers, and long beakers with the procreative drive built into them procreate only with other long beakers.

We've learned in breeding, as with two fast running horses, that when we get two of an eccentric type, we tend to concentrate their genes with the probability of producing faster and faster running horses by breeding them together. But as you develop a special concentration of genes, you do so at the cost of breeding out general adaptability, and then your hybrid has to be protected. There are other things that you have to do for it that it used to do for itself.

It is also to be observed in the general pattern of our energy universe that, because the local systems are always giving off energies in diffused ways— every local system changing, transforming, moving, giving off its energies in diffused ways—we have an expanding universe. Because the universe is more or less increasingly disorderly (with a consequent distribution of energies into smaller and smaller packages), the number of times that you encounter small amounts of energy that can do small things is very much greater than the number of times you encounter large amounts of energy that do large things—there are more mosquitoes than there are earthquakes. This is just the general nature of the universe. Consequently, encountering a very large amount of energy, such as a star, would be a very remote possibility for much of the universe. This means that the large events in the environment are relatively infrequent. This being so, in losing general adaptability there is a tendency to lose those capabilities which are in reserve for only the very occasional, but also very important, big things. The birds I spoke about developed longer and longer beaks. Suddenly there is a great marsh fire and these birds discover for the first time that their beaks are so heavy they can no longer fly. That's where the extinction comes in—as a consequence of overspecialization and a resulting loss of general adaptability.

Our human society, by becoming more and more specialized, has been getting itself into a very precarious position. Although we've developed the ability to use the energy of the atom to perform extraordinarily large tasks, we have in effect no world authority on what we ought to do with this ability. We have no fundamental authority on how we'll use our energies in important and constructive ways. And we find our energies are being developed in enormous ways for no better purpose than to destroy man. By now we are, by way of retaliatory button pushing, technologically capable of eliminating man from the earth.

Since we've been getting into serious trouble as a result of our specialization, I'd like to know how it happened. We were designed, obviously, to be generally adaptive, and yet we have become specialists. As I contemplate this educational institution of higher learning, Auburn, and indeed all educational institutions, I'm trying to discover the trends, the possible modifications in our educational processes, that may be highly desirable. All universities are organized today on the working assumption that specialization is essential. Now how did *that* come about?

Universities are quite new in the history of man. The technical ones go back to military undertakings and the like. Looking back in history, I find that there were some very strong men and there were some very illiterate strong men. Now, in that situation, if you are the strongest man around and everybody is illiterate, and you find there is very little to sustain life, and that the drive to satisfy hunger and thirst and the desire to reproduce are very powerful, then you are simply going to say, "Well, it's quite clearly you or me, and I guess it's going to have to be you." And that's the way it was.

The strong man was able to organize himself into a powerful position by making it perfectly clear that he was stronger than that other fellow. Then came the followers who said, "Well, I'd better go along with him because he seems to be able to organize things here. Everybody gets out of his way and lets him have those things that are necessary to survive."

For life to be regenerated on earth, it must be supplied with energy. We are energy processes; entropy is always working. We have to take on more energy than we give off, because we don't have 100 percent efficiency in our use of energy. Now the only source of the energy needed to keep life going on board our little planet is the sun, which has been superbly designed in the right proximity to give us radiation without burning us up. Our biosphere is designed to refract those energies and separate them out into very useful frequencies. But you and I can't go out in the sun without our clothes and expect to get enough energy through our skin to keep us going. Vegetation has been designed to help do that. If we went farther out into the biosphere, beyond the Van Allen belts, we would get plenty of radiation, but we would die because such a radiation concentration would be fatal.

The vegetation just mentioned—the green vegetation on land and the algae in the oceans—is designed to impound energy. The land vegetation is beautifully water-cooled and has roots so it can get the water as moisture running through it to be able to take on all that radiation. It then impounds the energy by photosynthesis. You and I can't eat all the grasses and trees and bark; in fact, we can eat very little of those kinds of vegetation. But there are insects and animals that can. And so, as illiterate primitive man observes his drive to eat and the elements that sustain him, he sees a lot of people getting killed by eating the wrong mushrooms and the wrong berries and the wrong leaves and the wrong grasses. But then he sees the animals eating those same things not getting killed, and he decides that the animal is probably safe because the animal could digest it. Then he finds that he can live longer on the flesh of those animals with much greater safety. So the illiterate man goes after those animals for the flesh to regenerate himself. Where there are relatively few animals and a strong man, he says, "Now, I have my gang of strong men around me, and there are other gangs over here; now all those animals belong to me, you understand." Weaker people, those who weren't the king's men, had to make do with roots, berries, and herbs.

Now when you get that kind of a picture, we find that the strong man with his strong men around him operating with cunning and great strength had to have a little more cunning than the other strong men. If you get to be top man, then

there's something you have to do: you have to
work at it continually, to keep on being top man.
We see this operative in all animals, in all creatures,
in the battle of the male goats, the battle of the
bulls to see which one is going to be on top. It
goes on all through nature. But even the top man
has to sleep every once in a while. So he gathers
these very dull but strong men around him and
says, "Now, you understand that the greatest virtue
in the world—do you know what it is?—well, it's
loyalty. Have you got that good and straight? Okay,
so now I'm going to go and get a little sleep."

Even so, he was always aware that there were
some bright ones around who were not quite so
strong physically but seemed able to contrive
things—they could see things—they seemed to catch
on. So he said, "I think you're a bit too bright for
your own good, young man, and you're not very
big either. Maybe I'm going to have to cut your
head off."

And the bright young man replied, "Sir, I think
you could use my head in other ways. I can tell
you what your enemies over there are doing because I just happen to speak their language, and
I've heard what they were saying, sir."

"Very good, young man, a very good idea. From
now on your job is just exactly that. You concentrate on getting that information for me, and you
keep right at it."

And then somebody else said, "Sir, I think you

could use my head too. I know how to make a little better sword."

"Very good. From now on you're going to be my sword maker." And another smart young man was going to record the history, while still another was going to sing songs about how great the great man was. So the top man gradually developed this kind of bait capability just as, when he captured prisoners, he found out what they could do and what they knew as specialists. And he began then to develop little tutors. For example, the Romans and Greeks turned some of their war prisoners into tutors—into specialists for these special people.

Now, if you are the head man and you have this problem of feeding your own soldiers, your great capital capability, of course, is your strength, and beyond that is the food that you control. So you say, in order to have this man be a specialist with a tutor to make him even brighter—the better to outdo your enemy—you're going to have to feed both the scholar and his tutor. You have to take some of the food at your command and invest it in the process.

The pattern, then, is one of the head man saying, "All right now, you mind your own business, you understand, and you mind your own business, and you mind your own business. I'm the only one who minds everybody's business. Is that quite clear? Okay!"

Now, this is where specialization begins. I've just given you the scheme and the strategy and the design of Oxford University. The head man had his boys, and he wanted them to be comprehensivists, but he also wanted them to get used to these specialists and so he sent them to the same school. And the nobleman needed his chief soldiers to grow up and understand, too, and so he sent them off to school, along with those specialists. This is the way it began.

What we call specialization is really just brain slavery—just brain slaves. It is very important for us to realize this. We have had some extraordinarily powerful, brilliant head men in history.

In the big pattern of man on earth, we observe two very important environments—the land and the sea. Man typically considers himself a dry land creature—he finds that either he doesn't know how to swim or, if he can stay under water, he can't stay under water very long. So he thinks of himself as a dry land creature. But only a quarter of the total earth sphere is dry land, and not all is by any manner or means favorable for the sustaining of life. In fact, when we get down to what land would be able to sustain life, we find a very small percentage, only about two percent of the total surface scattered about the earth; and the people in some of these small increments do not know about the people in the others. A relatively few men discover favorable points for the sustaining or regenerating of their life. They don't invent these things—they don't invent any of the process at all. They just discover. And they find themselves beset periodically by wandering people who haven't been so lucky, who haven't found the good places, or who've exhausted their local resources and have now gone looking for a new place. Suddenly they come to some men who are successful; and they immediately say, "Well, it's going to be those people or ourselves." Then there is a battle, with the ones who found a way to survive having to defend their position.

The great historical strategy is very clear. First they tried the great walls, such as the one in China. But it was too much to mount, and it couldn't cover all the length. So they built smaller walls as a fortress, picking an area where there was water—a well—to be sure of having a supply. You must have water inside your fortress. When we get something like Mycenae, we find long passages down from the mountain heights, down secret passages in the rocks where one could get down fairly well. Then you built great granaries, and your farmers stay outside farming, so you don't get too confined; then, when the enemy is reported as approaching, you take everything out of the fields—you harvest all crops and put them all inside. Anything that can be stored is stored, the rest you just burn. When the enemy comes, you are all inside with food and water to last for a long time. People outside haven't been eating for quite awhile—they are already starved and weak. So you just watch them out there—just watch them get weaker and weaker. And you wait until they are weak enough and then you go out and kill them. That was the great scheme.

Now, under those circumstances, the heavier and higher, wider, more formidable the walls, the more secure; the bigger the granary, the more secure; security was in bigness, enormity. So they build a rock fortress, and they pick rocks to build the fortress.

While 99.9 percent of humanity is living that kind of life, there are people who have found a way of life on the river, the lakes, the waterfronts, the sea. But if you go out very far you begin to get into trouble. Gradually, better and better boats develop, and finally the round-bottom ship emerges that keeps stable on the sea. Earlier—as we know today—there were canoes and outriggers and dugouts that were able to travel great distances, but they couldn't carry any important kind of cargo. Men finally put several of those together and got a raft, such as did the early Polynesians, but even rafts were not good for cargo. The seas would roll over them and the food would spoil. Not until the deep-bottom boats could large amounts of cargo be carried.

Gradually, the explorers were making discoveries great distances away, going off to sea where they discovered that resources are very unevenly distributed and that climates vary greatly. By going to places that nobody at home knew anything about, they were able to bring back some extraordinary things which would complement what they had at home. Things they had at home that had seemed absolutely useless could be complemented by what they found elsewhere to create great new wealth. They discovered that just one good voyage could make a fortune.

Now then, in going to sea, you soon discover that stone sinks and wood floats. So when building your boat, you had better start with wood. Then you learn that making a wood and skin boat is even lighter and better than trying to hollow out the logs, and it would have great buoyancy, and you could put great cargoes inside it. Then gradually you learn about floatability—how much cargo you can carry—just by seeing your boat being laden down. Finally, you have Archimedes explaining the principle of displacement. Men then knew what the cubage of the ship must be for it to float—that is, equivalent to the cubage of water displaced times the weight of water per cube—and that is the weight of your ship and all the cargo that it can carry.

You have the men going to sea, encountering a very extraordinary kind of fundamental problem. In the first place, when you go to sea the conditions are fundamentally different. On the land, theoretically, you can close the blinds, you have your walls (in a deep-walled building), and you can put on your shutters and lock yourself up. It's night, you don't know what's going on, so you just shut yourself up good and safe. At sea, you can't shut the sea down. On land, it's possible to live a 12-hour kind of experience; living on the sea is a 24-hour experience. On land floods come and go; on the sea you *start* with flood and have it with you all the time. Waves on the sea are what we call seaquakes; they have the same characteristic as earthquakes on the land. But seaquake waves are much bigger than earthquake waves, and you have seaquakes every few days. When the waves are big enough to crash down over the deck, you have the equivalent of an avalanche. Men at sea have to cope with nature under extreme conditions: the kind of conditions men might face on land only once in a lifetime occur repeatedly in just a week on the sea. There is a great acceleration of high energy events.

In going to sea, then, you develop a ship that can get you there and back safely while being large enough to carry great cargoes. You need a good deal of advance information about the probability of finding valuable things after you get where you're going. And you have to know how to get from here to there because there is no land in sight: you have to learn how to employ the stars.

You have to invent navigation, and to do that you have to invent mathematics. I am quite confident that all the really important mathematics, certainly the trigonometry between two stars and yourself, came out of this necessity.

The men who develop their capabilities in this way become brilliant. They have to be extremely tough and powerful men in order even to get their ship built. It is too big a ship for one man to build, and they have to have the power to say, "I command all the very good woodworkers in the kingdom to work on my ship, and all the people who know how to handle fabric are going to make my sails, and all the metal workers are also going to have to work for me. And they all have to be fed, so you farmers understand you're shipping all this food over to my shipyard to take care of these people, you understand pretty clear!" This kind of man, a man who is used to commanding other human beings and to maintaining his position physically, has to have a brilliant head, has to organize and discipline himself, and has to develop mathematics.

Now this man's purpose is to make a voyage and come back with great riches. His enemy over here knows this and says, "That's a pretty good idea that man has. I don't know just where he went, but I do know that when he comes back he'll be bringing a lot of valuable stuff. So all I've got to do is build myself a small boat, get some of my tough boys together, and the night before he arrives home we'll take his cargo away from him." So that became a very popular sport, too.

When we get out on the high sea, there's no way to enforce the laws that apply on land. Three-quarters of the earth was outside the jurisdiction of man-made laws. The men who went in for the seafaring life were inherently outlaws. The only law that had to be obeyed was natural law, and the question was, "Who is going to stay on top and who is going to go to the bottom?" Nobody on the land ever knew anything about it. And that's the way it was.

You learned to build the very best ship you could at home, using local resources—the best tree you had, the best fibre for your rope, and so forth. But you knew from previous voyages that, when you came to the next land, there were going to be some very taller trees with very much longer, stronger fibre; so you put in the better mast. Then you came to another country, such as the Philippines where you found much stronger fibre, and you took those fibres to make your ropes. In still another place, you found better fabrics for your sails. And so, as you sailed round the world, your ship got stronger and better. This was the beginning, really, of what we call the production line. And as you came to those places, you took some additional amount of those woods, and spars, and metals, and fibres and brought them home to build even greater ships. So a regenerative process begins in terms of the widely dispersed resources of the world.

Now if you have the same size ship as your pirate enemy but your mast is of stronger wood, your sail of better fabric, and your ropes of stronger fibre—then you can keep sail on when he has to take it off—when the wind begins to really blow. This enables you to outmaneuver him, and down he goes to the bottom. Thus the man who had a greater amount of floatability, who could do more with less, was the one who would stay on top. This was the very essence of shipbuilding technique.

You find these resources around the world, and what is unique about each one is that each could do a little more of some special task. So you design special tools that do specific things in more effective ways, but always it's doing more with less, always the ratio of the investment of weight to the time or the energy in the muscles of the men who put the sails on and off. You have pounds, watts, and seconds to invest. Whoever could get the most out of those pounds, watts, and seconds was going to run the world. So this was where the great trail was, out beyond the laws of people on lands.

Out there men became extraordinarily powerful, and in time they learned the strategy that several ships can outmaneuver one ship. You can box in your enemy or the prize you want to protect; so navies were invented. And you learn to divide and conquer. Now divide-and-conquer or divide-and-rule was something I alluded to when explaining the origins of education specialization, where the head man learns that divide-and-conquer is very powerful indeed, and that anticipatory divide-and-conquer. Divide and conquer the others before conquer is more effective than tardy divide-and-they even know they're being divided. And that's exactly what the top man was doing when he took in all the bright ones and made them specialists. He didn't bother with the dull ones at all. The bright ones weren't allowed to talk to one another very much, and in time they became so specialized, and their languages so different, that they couldn't talk to one another anyway.

In developing comprehensive navies, the top men had to build new ships. They chose the great big patterns—they began to deal in the total world as they knew it. If you were an invisible world master of the water-ocean earth, you had to maintain the capability to create and run the best world navies. You had to have physical control of the biggest patterns. No matter what else we may think of these men today, they were magnificently imaginative big-scale operators. They had to use all that their science had learned about energy in order to give their navies the faster, farther, more accurate hitting power needed to stay in supreme command of the physical affairs of mankind. This involved not only designing the network of world-around voyaging and the ships for each task, but also designing the industrial establishments and world-around mining operations and naval-base building for production and maintenance of the ships. This top-man planning inaugurated the large scale thinking of the world-around industrialists of today.

You may wonder: "Aren't you talking about the British Empire?" and I answer: "No." The so-called British Empire was a manifest of the world-around misconception of who ran things and a disclosure of the popular ignorance of absolute world control by a few top men through their local stooge-sovereigns and their prime ministers, only modified innocuously and locally here and there by the separate sovereignty's internal demo-cratic processes.

As we soon shall see, the British Isles—a fleet of "unsinkable ships" and naval bases commanding the great harbors of Europe—were the possessions of a few top men who sailed the seas. Since these men were building, maintaining, and supplying their ships on those islands, they quite logically gathered up their crews from among the islanders, who were simply seized or commanded aboard by royal edict. Seeing these British islanders on these ships, people around the world mistakenly assumed that the world conquest by these few top men was a conquest by the will, ambition, and organization of the British people. Thus the grand deception of a few top men emerged victorious. The bulk of the British islanders never had any special desire to go out and conquer the world, but as a people they were manipulated by the top men and taught to cheer when informed of "their" nation's world prowess.

The British Isles were themselves unsinkable flagships, commanding all the harbors of all the customers. Whoever ran those islands was going to run the world. They were not only situated in a commanding position, but they had large supplies of the woods, the metals, and other things needed to build ships. The fighting over those Isles by the Vikings, by the men of Europe, made the shores of these islands one continuous battle ground for little pirates trying to become big pirates. The same can be said of Scotland. Gradually there emerged the most powerful people who kept things under control everywhere, with the British Isles as the terminal. These people are normally water people: their home was the sea—and in fact, then, their home was the world. Water people are inherently world people because three-quarters of the earth is water, and the waters go everywhere. Land people are inherently "local," water people inherently "world."

As I've said, there are two completely different worlds operative, one on land, one on the sea. In the latter, experiences accelerate very rapidly, and so water people have had occasion to invent more powerful tools much more frequently than land people have had. Of course, the development of new strategic tools must be kept completely secret. It is a very interesting fact that none of the great naval organizations, such as the Navy department of our own United States or the British admiralty, kept records of the engineering work that went into their ships. Such records were quickly and methodically destroyed. You got your ship in operation *before* the enemy could find out just how you were able to do so much more with so much less, since it was your doing that more with less, which meant you were going to run the world. It is a hard, tough, ruthless game, and the point of it is that our land society, up to now, had been organized in terms of the bigger the security, the bigger and higher the walls and the bigger the grain bin. On land man had not learned to make do with a light structure on a really great venture.

The results of sea technology were completely to be expected. Its acceleration brought men of the sea into steam ships and into metal ships and then into ships of the air. This is where it really ends, with the ship of the air or the airplane, because in 1929 a single little airplane with a torpedo was able to sink a large armored cruiser. It was really the end of the supremacy of the ship.

The year 1929 happened to coincide with another very important set of events. We had what I call the "in-pirates" and the "out-pirates." The in-pirates, with their navies, were something like the British admiralty, and while command of the seas seemed to belong to one country, it was, as I explained, really simply a matter of convenience to have that country as a terminal.

Actually, the in-pirates invented what we know today as countries. All of what we know as historical countries were invented by these top strong men. When they came to a country they said: "I am dealing with the head man here, you seem to be the toughest guy and now I have my ship and I can carry much bigger cargoes than you can carry on the backs of your men or on the backs of animals. I have the great line of supply." In warfare, remember, you have that business of the seige, when the side that continues to eat is the one that will be able to come out and do some decimating.

So we find the great powers coming to various geographical areas such as the one we now call Italy. Now in Italy, there were hundreds of strong local barons with their castles, counting their little local farms. And the top man of a great power said: "I see they have a lot of these local strong men around here. I don't want to be bothered with them. So I'm going to make you *my* strong man. I have my ship and I have the line of supply, and I'll see that you get your food. You just go and beseige those castles. You used to be starved. You're not going to be anymore, because I have my ships and I can see that you get all the food you need. Now this is a narrow piece of land; I'll bring my ship around to this side and get right near that castle. You are going to eat. The people inside there think they are pretty secure, but you're going to keep getting food all the time and they are going to use up all the food they have inside." That's exactly what happened. None of the walls of the great castles along the Rhine or in Italy had to be breached; the people inside were simply starved out by what I identified for you as another grand strategy—when the men began to master the world by mastering their ships. "From now on this is called Italy and you are the head man and I want you to wear a lot of purple and gold and make yourself very prominent because I am not at all worried about you people here on the land. But I am going to worry about those other pirates. And the pirate whom I must now go to fight is a pretty bad one."

The greatest strength the people of the sea had was in the fact that the sea was very big and you could get lost in a hurry. The other man didn't know where you were going, or when you were going, or why you were going, all of which made it very hard for him to intercept you. And the Earth is spherical: fourteen miles away you were what they call "down under" the horizon, so you could stalk your enemy under that horizon—if you had the faster and better ships. So the very essence of the men who were masters of the world was their secrecy. And that didn't mean fooling; a little joking to show off once in a while. They knew they wouldn't stay on top for long if they ever let people know who they were. That's why they wanted all those very prominent head stooges around who would seem to be powerful in their own right, why they created the heads of these great countries like Italy and gave them big names, distinctive colors, and so forth. But all of this was completely obscure to man on the land, of course, because it was intended that he not know about it.

We see this pattern developing up to the point when the pirates who listened to their scientists or specialists and put in steam suddenly found themselves way ahead of the other powers that were still waiting for wind to fill their sails. And then the scientists said: "Make your ship of steel because then you can drive it so much harder." The in-pirates did just that, and they did get way, way ahead of their competition. They carried much bigger cargoes. They got so far ahead of the out-pirates that they began to get a new kind of a pattern. The out-pirates just couldn't catch up to them now at all. However, in order to build the steel steamships, they had to take the marine railway and run it backwards up to the land. That is the beginning of the tunnels and the railways with steam power going up on the land to pull the great cargoes. For the first time, the way of distributing that load to be carried on land had to be balanced just as in the launching of the ship; a marine railway track, depending on one keel, has to have a double rail so she won't tip over. This is the time, also, when blast furnaces were developed, and it is a very strong history of world industrialization from here on. For example, steel was being made for ships of the sea for fifty years before anybody thought of putting a piece of steel into a building on land. Land people just weren't thinking about that kind of thing. They put steel into their ships and into their marine railway, but not into building on the land: stone and wood served well enough to keep the rain off. Again, in order to have that steel hull with the steam freight power, you had to have forced draft—the beginning of air conditioning. But to develop air-conditioners, there had to be good oxygen to clear the air going down there and you had to have light going down into places where there was no light at all. That meant generators and all manner of auxiliary equipment. And they had to have fresh water for their boilers; salt water wouldn't do.

So we had advanced invention realizations for

over a century on the sea before we had them on the land. We had refrigeration for ships at sea for about half a century before it came up on the land. All the great generators were built for the ships of the sea at first; it was only after the people on land had been organized to produce all the generators they could use on the ships that the manufacturers of these goods looked around for some new customers. So the men on land who owned the new kinds of equipment needed to produce steel, and electric generators, and so forth finally discovered that these things were also salable for use on land, and that they could make a new kind of profit they'd never thought of before, quite apart from what they were winning from their commerce of the sea. They became very, very deeply involved with this new kind of profit.

This is a very wonderful thing that they found, this mechanical cow. You just kept milking it. When some inventor came along and said: "I can show you a better way of doing it," they didn't like that at all, because they thought that their "then" mechanical cow was doing just fine. They were monopolizing everything and they didn't have any competition whatsoever, so there was no reason for changing once the mechanical cow was working and bringing in plenty of profits. A scientist came to the great powers and said: "Sir, I'll show you a way to make steel so that it won't rust."

But the great powers thought: "The more it rusts, the more I sell. How crazy can you get? Take the papers out of this man's pocket, he's obviously crazy. Put him in the insane asylum—and put those papers in my drawer here."

They were very worried about these people, the scientists, because when they asked them how they could do these things, they said: "Well, sir, it's done with mathematics like this and so forth."

And the pirates said: "Well, we don't understand mathematics, that must be very dangerous stuff." They reserved for themselves the right to be master. They judged and tested everything with their own eyes, their own noses, their own touch, their own hearing.

The in-pirates got very, very far ahead of the out-pirates, until finally the out-pirates saw that man was putting all those papers in his drawer. Then they said: "Well, he got way ahead of us with the steam and steel business. It could be that these inventors and scientists are giving him lots of technology and he is paying no attention to it at all. Maybe if we could get those papers we just might be able to take him by surprise." And that's exactly what they did.

World War I, then, saw the out-pirates challenging the in-pirates' mastering of the surface of the sea. The out-pirates said: "We are going to go *under* the sea and *above* the sea to learn a new geometry of attack." And they found this new technology, the technology of the submarine, which enabled them to go under the sea and to break the in-pirates' line of supply to such an extent that the in-pirates almost lost. To save themselves, the in-pirates had to get that great productivity of tools which had been developed in the United States and all those untapped resources really to work on their side. And they had to let the American navy come up to parity with what we call the British navy, or what I have explained to you to be the navy of the great Masters of the World.

Now to do this, the in-pirates had to listen to the scientists. The other side had listened to scientists and had taken and used what the scientists had given them in order to get in position to challenge the in's. With the line of supply being broken badly by submarine attack, a scientist said to one of the high command in England: "Wouldn't it be just as good as getting twice as many guns to the front if we could make the guns that do get to the front last twice as long?"

And the high command told the great power: "You could really make those guns last twice as long and this would make up for these deficiencies."

And the great power said: "You've got to let those scientists get going there."

And so they did. They opened the Pandora's box of new technologies by letting science get going.

In World War I, these new technologies took us from wire to wireless, from track to trackless, from visible muscle structures to invisible alloy structures. In other words we went from the world of what we call "sensorial" reality into the great ranges of reality that are nontuneable directly by man's senses. Because of this, the great masters who did everything with their own senses could no longer know quite what was going on. The new technology did save the day: the in-pirates won their war. But when the war was over, the old masters undertook to do what they called getting things back to normal. They said: "Let's get things back to where we can see them," and they tried to do just that in the 1920's. But they couldn't turn things back to "normalcy." They didn't know what was going on. Suddenly they had lost by default.

"Twenty-nine" saw the folding-up of earth's old masters. Having always kept themselves secret, they certainly didn't announce their own demise. They even hoped it wasn't true. There was no public announcement of their passing because the public had never known that these masters existed. 1929—all the mills have stopped around the world, all the wheels have stopped, everything has stopped. We have people in Germany saying: "There's the iron, there's the coal, there's the blast furnace; we know how to make steel; why aren't we?" They asked their local politician: "Why don't we make steel?" They didn't know the local politi-

cian was only a stooge. But he did, and so he got
on the telephone and tried to reach the old master.
No answer. So suddenly the politicians saw they
were really up against the wall. They never had
had anything really to do with how to make the
world work, but the local people were now de-
manding that they do it. So they simply changed
their government, put over a new one, and started
opening those blast furnaces. And they started
demonstrating that there was something very powerful: that wealth really could be generated without their having money, that wealth was something
else which could produce the tools.

So, then, we have Hitler, and Hitler said: "Well,
the way we propose to run the world is to decimate
all the people we don't like." That is not a very
good solution—a very unhappy one, in fact. But
that is what they started to do.

In no time at all it was being said: "You have no
wealth and no money in Germany." Actually they
had real wealth—that is, they had productive
capability—and soon they were challenging the
whole world and almost knocking it off its feet
again.

We have, then, the beginning of the era of the
little man everywhere not knowing that there ever
were those great masters (now forsaken) and
identifying the success of those who were successful with the fact that they had more knowledge.

They were "better informed." So all the mothers

and fathers said: "I would like my boy not to have to go through the pain I've gone through, being illiterate and having a very poor vocabulary. If my boy had that schooling, he might really be able to get there."

The voice of common man had something to say that could be listened to. This voice had produced a Magna Carta and a Bill of Rights. We had then the representatives of democracy realizing the one sure way to be elected would be to give their constituents schools. And so they simply set up a prototype school of one of the great powers and copied that prototype. For years we couldn't have a school unless it was built in Georgian-style architecture, or something like it. Whatever Oxford had, we had to have. It was physically or superficially exactly the same picture. It was never thought out what education *might* be; we simply bought in wholesale lots the specialization of the old, dead great pirates.

That's how we got *our* specialization. We got all specialized, with everybody minding his own business—and now nobody can mind everybody else's business in order to put things together. That's where we are right now. We're all dressed up with enormous capability and absolutely no ability to coordinate the affairs of the earth.

These old great powers saw things in a very limited way, but they really were running the world. They ran it on a very clear pattern and things were very well coordinated. All our customs have been developed out of these patterns. But the great powers had some misinformation from their scientists. All the empires of man up to just yesterday were what I call infinite worlds. The Roman, Ghengis Khan's, and all those other ancient empires came into being when man thought of the world as an infinitely extended lateral plane with perhaps regions of mountains here and there and some valleys, but still a world that went out flat in all directions. There was the known area, which comprised the great empires, outside of which you came first to some pretty uncivilized people; and beyond, the dragons; and beyond them—well, you'd better not go any farther because it gets pretty dangerous. When you have an infinitely extended plane, then there is a possibility of an infinite number of variables. If you don't like what is going on here, there is always the chance that out beyond the known and towards infinity you can find a roastbeef mountain or a mountain of gold or whatever it be. Man could choose his own god because an infinite number of gods could exist. Just shop around for the right one and you'll come out all right.

This was the condition of things up to the time of what we call the British Empire. This empire—although we are not taught this in our history books—was the first spherical empire. Being spherical, it was a closed system—the first closed-system empire as compared to the open-system empires of before. Suddenly we have man discovering the utility of the closed system. With the closed system there are no longer an infinite number of variables. And this happened only a hundred and seventy years ago in 1800.

In 1810 we have Thomas Malthus, who was professor of political economics for the East India Company—those were the *really* top-grade in-pirates—and the first economist to receive the total statistics from around a closed-system world. He found it all quite astonishing and wrote in his first book that: "Apparently men are reproducing goods to support themselves." Ten years later, after receiving more data, he was able to say in his second book: "Apparently men are reproducing themselves at a geometrical rate and are only producing goods to support themselves at an arithmetical rate. Therefore, except for a chosen few, humanity is destined to be a complete failure."

Now during this same period the great powers were taking their geologists, biologists, and other scientists hither and yon around the spherical closed system to learn what resources could be found and where; they wanted the specialists to tell them what there was to be exploited and how it could be exploited. Among the biologists being taken around the world, Charles Darwin went to catalogue all the living species. By this work, Darwin discovered certain design interrelationships out of which he developed a theory of evolution. Now it's important to realize that Darwin could not have developed a theory of biological evolution for the Roman Empire, with its open system, because he would have had to include dragons to the nth power. You can't develop general system series unless you have a closed system. It is only quite recently, for less than two centuries, that we have had the advantage of closed-system information to work with.

Right on the heels of Malthus, then, Darwin came along with his theory of evolution based on the idea of the "survival only of the fittest." The in-pirates are getting this information from their intellectual slaves—and highly important information it is. What if you are the head man, at a point in history just a little over a hundred years ago, and Malthus and Darwin tell you that there isn't ever going to be enough to go around and that only the fittest are going to survive. The scientists have said it and made it very clear; this is the scientific law. So you say: "Well, I'm obviously the toughest and the fittest in *this* system, and I'm going to stay on top and survive."

In the meantime, however, that same information is becoming available to another scholar, Karl Marx, and he says: "Well, I think that the workers know how to handle that seed to get something out of the ground. The fisherman knows how to do his work. The craftsman knows how to do his work. These pirates are parasites and they wouldn't know what to do if the workers weren't there. They couldn't do this work. They're just simply exploiting the worker. Therefore, the workers are the fittest." There was nowhere nearly enough to go around so you have the two extremes: on the one hand, Marx with his workers; on the other, the great powers. All the other political ideologies are somewhere in between.

If you had been the head man and you had this information and you say, "What do we do? Notify all the world that there is nowhere nearly enough to go around?" Divide everything up evenly and let everybody die slowly together! An appalling idea. Or we might do what the Greeks did: we might decimate the excess. That's no longer considered becoming. Well, there is something we could do. There are all these people out here and they don't even *know* that there is not enough to go around. They're still thinking of infinity. They've got their gods, and while practically none of them is going to survive beyond about twenty-seven years of age, at least they're fairly content about it all, because their hopes spring eternal so long as there's a roastbeef mountain over there. So why disillusion them? At least let them have their hope. We know they're doomed to early death, but we'd be making things even worse if we told them the truth.

So that's exactly what they did, and that's what we call the "underdeveloped" countries, and that's what we're still doing about it today. The in-countries gradually found that they didn't know just how much there was to go around. "We can't guarantee that you are going to survive on our side." But there seemed to be tough ones on each side in the survival-of-the-fittest game. They are the tough, strong people, and they survive all right. And we join up with the other side—there seem to be enough for two sides. Two countries, three countries, four—there are alignments to see which side is going to survive.

In his early pattern of survival a man just picked up a stick or bludgeon. He was hungry and went out to fight. Later there were swords and still more swords as technology made enough of them. If you had a sword, you went out to fight with it. You learned early that you had better go out and fight to survive while you were still young and had hard muscles, because pretty soon you won't have those muscles and you've seen what has happened to those other boys who didn't do it while they could. They're just a miserable mess, rotting in the slums and dying very early.

Sometime later men got a little something better to fight with. They got their revolvers and were pretty busy with them—and that's really the gist of our western story. Most of the time in our western story a man could do some constructive work only once in a while—he was so busy with that revolver most of the time. Then suddenly they came up with bigger guns and ships that could carry them—bigger and bigger guns, the products of our science-directed technologies—just about the time that Malthus was making his discoveries.

Now we find both our sovereigns and our democracies saying: "Well, there are the different schemes of life. We think we've got a pretty good piece of land here, and we are going to defend it. We've also got a fairly good idea of how to get on with our enterprise. Man's primarily liberal, re-member, and quite evidently the best thing is for everybody to turn in his gun and spend a great deal of time looking out for himself. We will have a pro-fessional military who will look out for things; we'll have some agreement about our rules of playing the game so that you and I can get very busy and take care of raising vegetables. We can grow things or we can manufacture this tool, whatever it is."

So society organizes itself this way, because the man growing things and the man manufacturing things are both completely preoccupied with their work. But there had to be somebody looking out for their *joint* interests in the meantime—hence political systems. The picture is one of some people tilling their fields and looking to this year's crop, others managing their factories and concentrating on this year's production and customers, the politician looking out for just his particular constituents, and so forth. All these people are planning ahead for just one year, two years, or for possibly a crop rotation perhaps five years ahead. The politicians looking ahead only as far as the next election. With every one keeping eyes on his own work, all the looking is quite shortsighted in both time and geography. It's left to the military to keep watch on the world and to look far ahead to anticipate trouble. They'll get their big guns on the promise of looking out for us all when the official fighting time comes.

This was the scheme of things that began to prevail in a big way starting just a hundred and fifty years ago, more or less, and with it the military said quite clearly: "From this point on, our statecraft is predicated on Malthusian and Darwinian concepts, on the basic assumption that there isn't nearly enough to go around and there never will be." And this was the thinking up to the beginning of the present century. My father died when I was very young and I had a rich relative and he said: "Young man, I would like to tell you some things because I think your father would want me to do it. In the first place, I am rich and there are not many of us who are rich." (At that time there were not so many rich men as now.) He went on: "I am on the board of directors of a great many companies and between one thing and another, I have quite a lot of information." And he said: "I know you have been impressed with your grandmother's golden rule and you're going to feel badly about what I am saying here, but the fact is that if you want to bring up a family of five, the figures are that less than one in one hundred is going to be able to live out his potential life span. And if you want to be economically successful, the chances are about one in a million; these are the figures just now." He said: "Understand then, that it isn't just you or the other fellow, it is you or a hundred others. If you want to bring up a family of five you are going to have to deprive five hundred people of their right to live. Well, I know you don't like that. Don't tell your grandmother, but I've already taken care of her hundred."

Now, that's the way it was when I was already a grown man, so-called, and I didn't like that picture at all. I thought this was a pretty messy situation but that was the very essence of why we had a navy and everything else in the system. So the scheme was that the military, and particularly the navy, which could carry loads too great for the backs of horses over land, would control not merely the local last-defense but the big story which was the world. It really amounted to this: Whoever could deliver the greatest hitting power the greatest distance in the fastest time with the greatest accuracy and the least effort is going to be the side that eats. The other side is going to die. Now death may be slow or may be fast; you may be killed outright in war or may just die slowly in a slum, which is really a much worse and a more humiliating kind of life.

This is the way things were organized. The military said this accurate hitting power is a matter of science and we need chemists and physicists and mathematicians. And this need brought about and was really the beginning of the great technical schools. Science formed military usage, and the military has been the prime underwriter of almost everything we call science. The spies said: "Well, well, the scientists on the other side are escalating," and then new orders were issued. "All right, scientists, you've got to get up to here now"—all giving rise to rapid escalation of scientific capabilities on both sides.

Now I'm going to point out to you something about technology. I'll go back to 1810—to the time of the first economic census in the United States. At that time there were a million American families and our total wealth, including wilderness, all public lands, homesteaders, and the rest, was about $3,000 per family, or about three billion dollars. What would have happened in 1810 if we had chosen the ablest, wisest, and most trustworthy of our citizens and said: "Gentlemen, we would like you to form a planning committee to take our three billion dollars and, as rapidly as possible, employ our total resources in the most intelligent way we know how, to take care of the most people in the shortest time." As it happened, in 1810 we were not too far from inventing the telegraph. Suppose our forefathers had said: "We are going to undertake not only to develop a telegraph, but we also are going to send power through a solid wire. [Nobody had ever heard of such a thing!] We are then going to go even further and have wireless; we are going to have all the things that we have today: the periodic table, the discovery of atoms, etc." What would have happened if a man had said: "We are going to develop transistors and go around to the other side of the moon?" In 1810, they would have said: "Too bad we picked this fellow for the committee; we'll obviously have to replace him." There's not one item of modern technology that we've acquired since 1810 that would have been possibly accredited or even dreamt of. And if they had known what it was going to cost. . . ! If they had asked the committee: "What is it going to cost to get those things?" and someone had said: "it will cost about a quadrillion dollars"—obviously he would have been disqualified too.

But what *really* happened was that a moment came when the great pirates realized that the out-pirates were really pushing themselves forward. This is often found in a political situation when local politicians find conditions getting unbearable. Looking out for their own side, they set conditions guarded by fences to try to make their own side survive.

Finally it comes to an impasse and there is going to be a war. So the politicians say to the military: "All right, we're going to have to have a war. What are you going to need?"

The military says: "Well, our side has leveled off here, but our spies tell us the other side is going to start at this higher level of technology. They are going to be able to fire five or ten thousand yards, whatever it is, with great accuracy."

Naturally the politicians want to know: "What's it going to cost to beat them?" and when they hear the answer: "We don't have that kind of money. We can't afford it."

The military says: "Buy or die."

"Can you produce?"

"Yes, we can produce."

"Well, no telling how we'll ever pay for it, but go ahead and produce it."

And that's what we did. That's how we've acquired all this technology. Acquiring it, then, we quickly come to a World War I and II. Up to this time wars had been in the era of agriculture which took farmers from their farms, used up food supplies, devastated the fields. Everybody suffered. World War I was an entirely new kind of war, however, because it related to this bigger pattern

I've given you, with the navy and all those resources around the world which could do very special things with new-found techniques. It was what I call an energy war. To explain, I shall have to digress.

I spoke to you earlier about man's developing tools. Just as my own personal strategy, I found that I could divide all tools into two main classes—craft tools and industrial tools. By craft tools I means those that could be invented, produced, and operated by one man starting nakedly in the wilderness where he could pick up a stick, for example, and use it as a spear. This category includes all kinds of tools for working stone and so forth. All the great artifact heaps that we find around the world are tools that could be and probably were invented by some one man, starting from nothing in the wilderness with no information from anybody and using just his own experience, which taught him that this thing just might work. He tried it and it did work.

By industrial tools I mean the ones that couldn't be produced by one man. That's a simple enough cleavage. The first industrial tool was the spoken word. You can't invent a word without two people. It's very interesting. You have no occasion to invent a word without two people. So, as the Bible says: "In the beginning was the Word." I'll say: "In the beginning of industrialization was the word." This is the beginning of relaying information and experiences from one man to another. Because men were able to relay information both in terms of overlapping lives and also travel, they began to consolidate all kinds of information. And we get then to the industrial tools that clearly fit my definition; for instance, the steamship *Queen Mary,* obviously a tool that could not possibly have been produced by one man or run by one man, or used by one man. The telephone system, a roadway system, great blast furnaces, and so forth—all these industrial tools are very extraordinary things that can accommodate you and me. They are the consequence of all the information from all the history of man about all resources everywhere, and their superiority over the craft tool is very, very great. They involve discovery in the scenery around us: whether in that rock there is something called beryllium and that beryllium can make you a coil spring that won't fatigue or spout; or that there are such things as chrome and nickel, the addition of which to iron produces a steel with a tensile strength a thousand times that of the tensile strength of iron alone. These are the kinds of thing that man found. And because of discovering that you could do more and more with less and less, a given cross-section could have greater and greater tensile strength.

So, out of this industrialization came the ability to do very large things in very big ways. But I'd

like to get down to something rather more fundamental. What man then has to discover is generalized principles. In literature, the word "generalization" means trying to cover too much terri-
tory too thinly. In science, the word refers to the
discovery of a principle that holds true in every
case; if you find even a single exception, then it is
no longer a generalized principle in science.

Consider, in ancient times, a man like any of us
going through the woods from time to time, woods
where men have not gone very often. Trees, fallen
in great storms, are strewn across one another, and
he tries to reach his destination as directly as he
can by climbing over them. As he climbs over one
of the trees, it begins to sink with him slowly and
he moves back for a moment and then comes up
again to the same place. As he walks on the tree
and it sinks lower and lower, he wonders what's
going on. He looks at the tree and *sees* that it's
lying across another one, the other end of which is
under a very big tree—and as he moves out farther
that enormous tree is being lifted, and he says: "I
never lifted a tree like that." He goes over and
tries to lift it with his muscle and finds that he
can't budge it. But standing back on the fallen tree,
sure enough he can lift it. Now I suspect this man
must have gone to his family with talk of a magic
tree, a very special tree that would be brought
home and kept around for a number of generations.
But then one day someone must have found that

any tree would do. Now, as a generalization, that is the beginning of the lever.

With that lever, man was able to move things he couldn't move with his own muscle. He began to move large rocks around and develop monumental defenses. Then the great pirates began to use levers in big ways. They set their slaves to rowing ships, which now could go windward with the rowing ship (something the wind alone would not let them do). They then began to have very much bigger ships, and they had to find a way to anchor them. The anchor, which of course had to be recovered when not in use, was made of metal and was very heavy. So they developed those same levers into a capstan around a shaft that the slaves pushed around horizontally—and up came the anchor. Later, man found that he could turn the shaft around vertically and from this came water wheels. Man had time and again felt the potential force of falling water (under waterfalls and so forth). Now men mounted a wheel on a shaft and bearings, and they put pulleys and then belts up into buildings to do all kinds of work. This was the beginning of man's discovering generalized principles and using them to channel energies from the atmosphere. In this case, the sun is elevating water out of the sea into the sky until it returns down the hills to be channeled to the ends of levers to do man's work. From this point on, the big task of man was to use his mind to find ways of doing work very much greater than his muscles could possibly do, by mastering and channeling energies of the universe onto the ends of levers.

The beginning is really World War I—the first big industrial war using big industrial tools. Here man shunted energies into the ends of levers in an enormous way. The way you get the most energy from any one place to another in the greatest amount and in the greatest hurry is by wire, which is much faster than by pipeline or tanker. In World War I, copper was used because it was the most plentiful of the metals and was a good conductor. In just one year, 1917, man mined and put to work more copper than he had in the whole of man's history before—an idea of the magnitude of the energy undertakings in World War I. He had two new technical capabilities, flotation and electrolytics, refinements that made it possible to get that copper to work very much faster. Since that time, man has been using copper in new magnitudes. But when the war was over and that wire was mounted on those poles it kept right on conducting electricity. What we had done was to rearrange the environment. We had taken the copper out of the earth and we put it to use where we wanted.

Because we had developed a production capability by landing energies on the ends of those levers, we were generating great wealth—and we kept right on doing so when the war was over. America and the rest of the world didn't quite understand all that wealth. Many said that there must be a lot of corruption in America because here the war was over and suddenly there were a lot of millionaires. During World War II, too, America was lend-leasing etc., using and giving away all manner of things, but still we came out of the war vastly richer than we had been, despite all the things we had done, all the ships sunk, and the rest. But even from those sunken ships we have been recovering the metals used to make them. This is an entirely new aspect to our world—that all metals that get mined, even if they are used to make something that becomes obsolete, are scrapped and then put right back into circulation. Of all the copper mined in the history of man, in fact, only about fourteen percent has gone out of circulation. The rest gets melted up and used over and over again. And every time we use it, the wire carries more messages-per-cross-section than it did before. We continually up the performance-per-pound as we reuse those metals.

An entirely new possibility for man is clearly emerging as a result of fallout from technology developed primarily for war purposes between 1900 and today. As compared to less than one percent in 1900, more than forty percent of the world's people have a higher material standard of living than could have seemed possible before the turn of the century. Not as a result of any consciously organized work on man's part—but rather as "fallout" of man's acquiring greater productive capability, under the aegis of fear of the great Armageddon, and without any understanding of what wealth really is or what he could "afford." Man thought that what he could afford was something held by the powerful man. The powerful man had something he called capital with which to finance his undertakings; if he said he didn't have the necessary capital, then he couldn't "afford" it. In these last statements, there is no realization of what wealth really is. Our understanding or lack of understanding of this point—what wealth really is—will have a whole lot to do with whether or not man is going to survive on the face of this earth.

Long ago, now, scientists had discovered from their studies of steam etc. what they called thermodynamics. There they found that every system always tends to lose energy. This is called entropy: systems run down. Thus when I went to Harvard as a student, that intellectual community was assuming that we all live in an "instant universe," just as Newton had. The stars were simply there—they always had been—and Newton's gravity operated instantly everywhere in the universe. If you have an instant universe, then this universe is a system and as such it must be losing energy and is, then, "running down." This was the way men were explaining things as recently as my student days. There had been some sun disturbance eons ago and the sun had thrown off light all right but ultimately we—the earth—would stop spinning for, as Newton said in his first law of motion: "A body persists in a state of rest, or in a line of motion except as affected by other bodies." His first statement, the "at rest," is the norm, and things are going to come to rest in the universe—eventually. If the universe is running down and energies are involved, then anybody who goes in for something new and uses up energies is anathema. This was when the great pirates were saying they didn't want any new inventions, because they had invested quite a lot to get those factories and they didn't want any change in their monopoly. As you can imagine, it was very easy to get scholarly support because they said: "Anybody who's using up that energy is 'spending' and helping the universe to 'run down' and die."

But then there had already been some experiments concerning speed-of-light measurements, around the turn of the century, and soon we have Einstein and Planck going even further and saying that the speed of light is 186,000 miles a second. They said it would take about eight minutes for the light to come to us from the sun, the nearest star to earth, and four years from the next nearest. As we now know, as we look around the sky we're seeing a live show taking place thirty thousand years ago, if we just shift the eye a little we see another live show taking place 150,000 years ago, and so forth. Therefore, Einstein and Planck said: "Well, the universe must be an aggregate of non-simultaneous and only partially overlapping events."

This is still the best description we have of the "universe." We see a little child growing bigger but certainly not running down and it's clear that a child is not entropic right from the time of birth. Thus, there are apparently areas where energies are accumulated. Einstein said that in this non-simultaneous aggregate of events, when energy is disassociated from one local system, it had to be associating into another. Exhaustive experiments, review of all experiments, and careful accounting of all further experiments made it perfectly clear that this was exactly what was going on—that when energy disassociated here it always associated there and was always a hundred percent accounted for. When there was any amount that wasn't readily accounted for, scientists began to discover that nature has some kinds of behavior that they hadn't experienced as yet, and that a lot of these kinds of energy behavior occur relatively seldom—hence man's not having run into them before. The scientist learned, then, to respect that fraction of the total that he didn't know about, and if he made further experiments and the same fraction was there, then he had to say: "Well, we don't know exactly what the behavior is but this is about the energy it takes, and we'll give it a name; we'll call it a meson." Still later, the scientists were actually able to isolate the meson and begin to find out what that behavior is. Even so, the experiment has disclosed neither the creation of new energy nor the loss of any of the existing. Energies, apparently, are finite and accountable. This law, the law of conservation of energy, states that energy cannot be lost, created, or destroyed. Which is simply to say that the working assumption of the best minds up to the time of the turn of the century, that the universe was running down, is no longer tenable.

This fact, that energy is not lost, has not yet found its way into our books on economics. In them we still find the word "spending"—a word referring to that now outdated thinking before man knew that there was a speed of light.

What, then, do we know about our wealth—about what we can "afford?" I think it is very important to ask this because you are quite a large audience. I've tried what I'm going to do with you now with several large audiences, the first time with fourteen hundred people at Stanford University, and later with fifteen hundred people at the Congress of American Planners, in Washington, D.C. According to a count I was given earlier, there are more than a thousand of you here tonight. Now I am going to propose several things to you and, if anyone disagrees with me, please put up your hand. I'm going to say to you, first, that no matter what you think wealth is, would you agree with me that no matter how much you have of it, you can't alter one iota of yesterday? No hands. Did you all hear it right? There are still no hands, and I assume everyone agrees that no matter how much wealth you have, no matter what you think wealth is, you can't change yesterday in any way. So we don't have to give any thought to yesterday as we try to think about what wealth is. Whatever wealth may be, it has to do with our now and our tomorrows but not our yesterdays. Consider now a man who has plenty of all the items we now say certify great wealth. This man has all his checkbooks, and all his stock certificates, and all his bonds, and all his deeds with him. He has a big stack of gold bars and a number of bags of diamonds with him. He's a certified billionaire—a billionaire on board a ship in the middle of the ocean. Suddenly the ship catches fire and all the life boats are burned and there this man is. If he hangs on to his gold he'll just sink a little faster than the others. They may be poorer in gold, but his kind of wealth can't give him any tomorrow either. So that kind of wealth isn't very powerful. If he could have gotten to the shore, he might have had some tomorrows, but he didn't have any way of doing that.

I would say, then, that what we probably mean by "wealth," really, has something to do with how many forward days we have arranged for our environment to take care of us and regenerate us in life and give us increased degrees of freedom.

Now, regeneration of life is produced first with energy, which we have in two fundamental conditions: energy associative as radiation that can be focused on the ends of levers etc.; and energy as radiation that can be converted into energy as mass or matter, and vice versa. Now we find that the energy part of the universe is conserved—that it cannot be created or destroyed—and we use the energy as matter for levers and energy as radiation to impinge on the ends of levers. This is really the fundamental great general scheme. Energy is conserved and there's plenty of it. Every time we rearrange our environment, we can get more energy and more levers to do more work to take care of the regeneration of more and more of our forward days. These energies are there, and they cannot be spent.

The other element of wealth to be defined is by far the more important. It is our intellectual capacity to recognize generalized principles that seem to be operative in the universe and to employ these principles. This is man's metaphysical capability, which we use to make an experiment to find out how the lever works and to discover generalized principles. There are a number of very important irreversibles to be discovered in our universe. One of them is that *every* time you make an experiment you learn more; quite literally, *you can not learn less*. That's a pretty interesting fact, isn't it, because it means that the metaphysical factor in wealth is one that is *always* gaining.

So we find the physical, or energy, component of wealth is being conserved and never will be lost, we find the metaphysical component to be gaining always—and wealth consists of these two. The weightless metaphysical and the physical—that's everything of the universe. I've left nothing out. That's all there is.

That wealth combines two factors—the physical which is conserved, the metaphysical which can only increase—isn't to be found in our textbooks, but it is what we are learning. It explains the fact that suddenly, completely to our surprise, we find forty percent of humanity prospering as no king ever dreamt of less than a century ago—in that yesterday we agree couldn't be repeated or changed. And it means that we are going to have to get into a completely new accounting system. There's not a single chapter in any book on economics about doing more with less. All the great secrets, how the world was run by the great powers —all carefully omitted from the books even now. And there is still no integration of the economists with the physicists in regard to the inner significance of these matters. The economists and physi-

cists are all too specialized. But these are the kinds
of things we are going to have to learn.

We are living on a closed-system earth, and yet
I find people asking, when they talk about space:
"Would you really like to be an astronaut?" "We
are all astronauts" I reply. "That's all we've ever
been." You say: "What does it feel like to travel in
space?" I say: "You tell me. That's all you've ever
been doing. Right now you are on board a spherical
space vehicle, only eight thousand miles in diameter, flying formation with our sun at a thousand miles a minute." That's a pretty good speed,
and yet people often say to me: "I don't know how
you travel so much," and I have to reply: "You
don't know what you've been doing." I hear people
say: "Never mind this space business; let's get down
to our problems here on earth, never mind all that
nonsense we've been spending our money for." I
simply say again: "You simply don't know what
you're doing. You're *already* on board a space ship."
So please don't ever say to me: "Let's get down to
earth." You're on board a space ship right now.
It's beautifully designed and man has been on
board it, according to present knowledge, for some
two million years. Utterly astounding, isn't it, for
us to be on board a space ship so superbly designed
and supplied as to allow man be be so utterly
ignorant for so long. And yet man is full of vanity

and false pride over his great success—forever patting himself on the back about "his" success when he didn't invent even one of those chemical elements. He merely discovered them, and fortunately each one of them shows him how to do something a great deal better. These are the things that have to do with our real education.

Now I ask you: "Is there anybody here who doesn't use the words 'up' and 'down'?" No hands. These words were invented to accommodate the concept that the world is a plane going out in infinity. In reference to such a plane all perpendiculars are parallel to each other, and therefore lines go in only two directions, up and down. But as man began to fly around his earth he felt that as an aviator he was not really upside down. He had to find better words, and so now he comes "in" for a landing and he goes "out" on takeoff or lift-off. From now on, then, please take the trouble to say to yourself: "I'm going outstairs and instairs." You'll soon begin to catch on that you're living on board a space ship, one on which the words "up" and "down" have no absolute meaning.

If there is an infinite system, then there are an infinite number of resources to be exploited. You can be just as careless and stupid as you want, since there are an infinite number of resources out there and we'll never run out. And there's an infinite amount of space in which you can get rid of all your filth as you waste all those resources. But in a closed system you can't do that—and that's the kind of system we're in. We have anything but an infinite number of resources! We have just enough to make the experiment. We're born utterly helpless —you needn't have an inferiority complex about being helpless or ignorant: every child is born that way. But the child is born with extraordinary, beautiful faculties that have not yet been laden with misinformation. What we are discovering, then, is that we are born utterly helpless, but with very good reason for our being born that way.

Part of the complementarity is that our spaceship is so well designed that we can be utterly helpless until we gradually learn that the important thing we have is here and now. We are all given this great chance to *learn*, and we've come to the point now, for example, where the pollution is getting so bad that very soon there will be enough dust floating in our sky to block out too much of the sun's radiation. When that happens, we won't be able to regenerate life on earth. And we're very close to that point of no return, in so many different ways. We've gotten to the critical point of whether man is really going to survive here or not. And we've only just come to the point of learning that since wealth can only increase, we can afford whatever we can produce: whatever we need, we can produce and we can afford. We don't have to ask anybody's permission! We've got to realize that this is so. Man is just coming out of a fantastic complex of slave thinking.

Now I would like to talk a bit more about the way I know what we all ought to know in relation to our experience. To begin: What do I mean by universe? I find that I must answer all my own questions in terms of my own experience, not in terms of what somebody said might be so, and using no axioms, no beliefs. I want to know: What have we learned by experience? In just this way, I shall answer: "I mean by universe the aggregate of all of humanity's consciously apprehended and communicated experience, whether communicated to one's self or to others." That's all I can possibly mean by universe. It's part of our experience, then, that all our experiences are as finite as our going to sleep and our waking up. Our smallest physical experiences get down to quanta. There is no continuum; there are no solids. We have separate energy packages, with everything in finite packages. Aggregates of finites are themselves finite. Our universe as defined is finite.

Another question: Does man have a function in the universe? Or is he just a theatergoer waiting to be pleased or displeased? I've made a discovery that seems to indicate that man does have a function, and that it is possibly one of the most important, even essential, functions in the system. But before I can go into this, I have to draw attention to a distinction that may seem a bit irrelevant at first— the distinction between mind and brain.

Now, I don't pretend to know what "mind" really means—or whether it has any meaning at all. But the physiologists and neurologists who have been probing the brain with electrodes over the last two decades have found out a great deal about this information processing, information storing/retrieving system of ours. Many fairly specific functions have been located in the brain. The men who have been doing the probing, the physiologists and neurologists, say that it is easy to explain all the data they have concerning this phenomenon if they assume two fine variables, one which they will call "brain," the other which they will call "mind." That is, it's easier to explain all the data they have discovered if they assume both a brain and a mind, than it is if they assume brain only. Why is this? It's because a telephone conversation going on over the system doesn't explain the feedback of the system itself. I've been thinking and exploring a good deal in this particular subject, and this last spring I was asked to give the principal address to the American Association of Neurosurgeons, two thousand of them meeting in Chicago. I offered them my differentiation between brain and mind and I received an ovation indicating that they approved of what I said on the matter, so I don't feel I'm misleading you in defining it for you now.

To make the differentiation between brain and mind, I'm going to go through the following: First, I'm going to start by saying, "I take a piece of rope and I start tensing this rope as vigorously as I know how and the more vigorously I tense it the tauter it becomes." Meaning that, if it is getting tauter, its girth is contracting; which means that while I am purposely tensing in one axis, at the same time and at 90 degrees to that axis, the rope is going into compression. I can also take a number of steel rods, long, thin, steel rods, which when I push at the ends bend rather readily. However, if I put a great many of them together in what is called "closest packing"—which is hexagonal packing: just as you put wires together to make wire rope in hex packing, and put a tension strap around those wires so they can't pull apart—I will have a tight bundle of rods. Therefore, it will act as a single column and I can load that column. As I load it on top, each rod would like to bend but can't because it is in closest packing: it can't bend inward because it will run into the other rods, it can't bend outward because of the tension straps. Therefore, as I load the rod bundle very heavily, it tends to become cigar-shaped. Its girth begins to increase and the wires around it begin to get stretched. So while I'm purposely loading my column in compression, at 90 degrees to my loading it is demonstrating tension. By such means it is very easy to demonstrate experimentally that tension and compression always and only co-exist.

A system is something that divides the universe into all that is inside the system as distinct from all that is outside of it. Your body is such a system. So is a tomato can. So is the earth. Viewed from inside, a system is concave; viewed from outside, it is convex. As the sums of the angles add up, the total is always less degrees than a plane. In order to take a flat piece of paper and make it into any kind of polyhedron, regular or irregular, you are going to have to keep taking out angles to bring it back to itself until, finally, it is a polyhedron. You always come into that concavity and convexity eventually. When energy radiation impinges on concavity, the radiation converges; energy impinging on convexity diverges the radiation. So concave and convex always-and-only co-exist. I give you three kinds of always-and-only co-existing functions: tension and compression, concave and convex, and proton and neutron. Now we can develop something we call the theory of functions where we have x and y as the two co-variables and have the x standing for tension, convex, and proton, and y standing for compression, concave, neutron.

Going further still, we come to something called relativity. And I can't have relativity without two variables to be related. Then I go further than

that. I have the word "universe." Now when I said
I take a piece of rope, I didn't have a piece of rope
at all, but nobody said: "You don't have a piece of
rope." I didn't say whether it was nylon or manila
or cotton or whatever. I didn't say what diameter
it was. This is called a first-degree generalization.
Everyone of you has had an enormous number of
experiences with ropes. I take a piece of rope as a
first-degree generalization. It is a second-degree
generalization to discover that tension and compression always-and-only co-exist. It's a third-degree
generalization—or a generalization-generalization—
to develop the theory of functions that embraces a
number of generalizations. It's a fourth-degree
generalization to say "relativity," a fifth-degree
generalization to say "universe."

Now a little dog will play with you a game of
tension and compression. He'll take hold of a belt
in his teeth, and there's compression in his teeth
and convex and concave surfaces in his teeth. And
he'll pull very hard on that rope—his protons and
neutrons all coordinating without his knowing it.
But there's certainly nothing in our experience
with dogs that tells us they will develop a theory
of functions. What the brain always deals with—
and neurologists agree with me—is special cases. It
remembers every special case or experience—that's
its wonderful recallability. But mind is the ability
to generalize. It is really quite wonderful to begin
to see the difference between these two, brain and

mind. And this generalization is utterly abstract, weightless, purely metaphysical.

As we look for a function of man in the universe, and remembering this realization, we recognize that the physical universe locally is giving off energies diffusely and in very random ways. So entropy is spoken of by the mathematician as an increase in the law of random elements. You find then that the physical is expanding and increasingly disorderly in the universe, and the therefore complex universe is expansive. Also as we have seen in physics, every fundamental behavior has its complementary. Therefore, there must be some phase of universe, where universe is contracting and increasingly orderly. We say, "Where is that?"

Now all the stars I observe are expansive and increasingly disorderly, giving off their radiations. We find, however, that our own little space ship, Earth, is receiving energy. The geophysical year showed daily receipts of many thousands of tons of stardust—radiation we receive every day from the sun and other stars. What is interesting about this is that the radiation doesn't just reflect off like a steel ball but is being impounded by radiation bending, just as you see the light bending if you put your pole down in the water. Radiation is bent the same way. The energy gets impounded as heat in the water. So we find our earth taking those energies and impounding them, for example, as

stardust and radiation heat. Also, vegetation impounds energy by photosynthesis, which means the
production of beautiful orderly little molecular
structures. This is the beginning of the orderly.
The biologicals are anti-entropical; all this chaos
suddenly being turned into order. What is very im-
pressive about all life is its inherently orderly
growth.

But of all the biologicals, human beings are the
only ones with mind function differentiated from
brain. If we took all the different rope experiences
this audience has had, I would say each one of
you must have experienced at least one hundred
kinds of rope, so that the total rope experience is
perhaps ten thousand kinds, and we've gotten that
down to only one piece of rope. Then we took all
the myriad kinds of experience with concaves and
convexes and with protons and neutrons; we got
that down into the theory of functions, and then we
embraced that even further, getting just the word
"relativity." And finally we got this word "universe."
What we have here is a pyramid of all the special
cases working up to generalizations, and generalizations to one word. That's as orderly as you can get.
We were looking for a phase of the universe where
things are contracting and increasingly orderly.
Nothing could be more orderly than those generalizations. We find, then, the metaphysical
balancing the physical—metaphysical apprehending, and ordering the physical. We find Einstein's

mind taking the measure of the physical, writing those beautiful, economical equations such as $E = MC^2$, saying that the physical universe is energy and you have to have one differentiation of energy on one side and another on the other side of the equation in order to understand it. And one is energy as associative matter, and the other is energy as disassociative radiation. And the rate of the radiation is to the second power or the rate of growth of a wave of 186,000 miles a second, to the second power. This tells us how much energy there was in that mass.

Here we have, then, intellect taking the measure of energy. We have nothing in our experience to suggest that this is reversible. Nothing suggests that energy will ever write the equation of intellect. I simply say to you that we have the metaphysical apprehending, comprehending, and ordering the physical. The physical tending to be disorderly and the metaphysical apprehending, comprehending, and putting together. Man, therefore, represents the very clearly demonstrated function in the universe that is essential to the regeneration of universe. Also we discover that the universe is a perpetual motion machine because its energy is never lost. So the minimum number of transformations is universe. It is the minimum and only perpetual motion machine, and perpetual conservation requires this metaphysical functioning of order and collection inherent to man.

We find, then, that man has this extraordinary kind of function, and what we have just discovered by all these experiments is that we really have this great function and were put aboard our space ship, Earth, to provide it. Where nature has an essential function, then she uses very great capability to be sure it persists—as, for instance, in the development of vegetation known to be able to regenerate life aboard this particular space vehicle. Vegetation has to regenerate its young, but it can't have its young if there is a shadow. The young plants would not be able to get any of the necessary radiation. Therefore, most vegetation launches its new life in little seeds on the winds and on the waters. The possibility of these seeds landing in just the places where they will prosper is poor, and nature makes many starts—enough to make sure that the species survives.

With metaphysical function essential to the continuance of the universe, nature is going to make many, many starts. From this reasoning we can assume that we are probably not the only group— that our little team of human beings aboard this space vehicle is not alone in carrying on this needed metaphysical function in the universe. Professor Fred Hoyle, the great astronomer in England, said that he does not feel he is misinforming society when he says there are probably hundreds of millions of planets with intelligent beings aboard. But whether our particular team is going to make good I believe to be very touch and go at this time in history. Everything we can be learning here of the progression and evolution is to make us aware of the vital need of insuring man's continuance and success aboard spaceship Earth.

Luckily I went to the U.S. Naval Academy during World War I when the in-pirates, in order to maintain their supremacy, had to let the American navy come to parity with them. There were barely two thousand men at the naval academy learning how the old great powers ran the world. Their studies deliberately made them comprehensivists— so they could be the right-hand men of the great powers. You were trained to be able to take all that had been found out about the physical universe and put it into all those tools of enormous tonnage. You had to be able to take all that hardware and go half-way around the world, and there was no way you could be communicated with about strategic matters faster than a courier could be taken by another ship. (Even though we had radio in World War I, we didn't trust it because the enemy could read cipher and code.) So you had to send commands by ship. Therefore, when you went off in a ship with all that expensive hardware, there was no central authority to tell you what to do. You had to be trained to be able to build new naval bases. You had to understand the whole pattern of the great ambitions, of how you run the world, and where the major commerce was, where all the resources were, how to handle people, and how to organize things in fundamental ways. So the training was designed to make a man a comprehensivist. And the very essence of being a comprehensivist is the following: you learn about those generalized principles, because it isn't a generalized principle if there is any single exception. Therefore, although there may be all kinds of names used by the specialists for a particular thing, you learn it's the same generalized principle.

I was science and technical editor of *Fortune* magazine for two years, 1938–1940. I was brought in to institute a new phase of their reporting because the general managing editor felt that the readers of *Fortune* ought to have a better understanding of the scientific foundations of their great corporations. My job was to make them aware of those scientific foundations. We had a month to prepare each story. I went with the researchers, who were all Ph.D.'s, to visit those companies. They were the ones who were going to write about the business side of things. I went there to organize the writing about the scientific side and I was usually given approximately a double spread or more in *Fortune* to tell that side of the story. The chief scientist, the vice-president in charge of research or whatever he might be called, would always say to me: "Your task is hopeless. Really to understand what we are doing here in depth, the only way it can be expressed is mathematically, and unless readers of *Fortune* read mathematics you cannot really communicate." For every issue, I was able within that one month to go in depth into that work with our scientists and to convert it back into conceptual language and to tell the *Fortune* reader in ways that even the chief scientists admitted were not just pleasant analogies but were efficient explanations. They always said that I had actually succeeded in telling faithfully and in depth what they were doing, and I was able then to demonstrate that my kind of training as a generalist made it possible for me to go in depth with any scientist into any subject in one month. I'll just simply say that in our society, then, you don't have to be that much a specialist. You can get that specialized kind of tutoring very rapidly today. You can become very sharp in any kind of subject if you have organized yourself well in terms of generalized principles. But there are still not many of us who can do it.

There are ninety-two regenerative chemical elements. There is multiplication and division of these elements, and you really must master the understanding of these fundamental transformations. I said that our society is on the way to extinction through man's overspecialization. Inad-

vertently, our society has developed its own anti-
body: the computer. And it has developed the
computer because it is getting ready for World
War III. It realizes the complexities of dealing
with all the different kinds of alloys and an entirely new way of looking at things that has been
coming since 1932, when for the first time we had
on the shelf the isolation of all the different chemical elements. We now can take the universe apart
and put it together again in preferred ways. We
used to have chance discovery of alloys; but suddenly, when we came to the space program, we
got to where we had to have a metal which could
take the re-entry heat and still hold together in
the right shape in addition to its other functions.
And so we had to invent those needed alloys. With
the space program, we've gone through an entirely
new era of our technology. We used to say: "You
can design things out of the materials that are
available," and all schools of architecture had
courses in materials. But now you can make the
needed materials without any intermediary form
of tubes and angle irons and sheets; you make the
end form instantly out of that special alloy without any intermediary nonsense.

We are well into an era of entirely new dealings
with our physical universe, into an advanced phase
of technology. Well, I'll only talk about what we've
developed already. When you think about an automobile, there are 5,000 different types of parts. A

residence has only about 500 types of parts. A great airplane has between 25,000 to 50,000 types of parts. In 1946, when we came out of World War II, one big corporation, International Harvester, had in inventory, in order to service all its different kinds of equipment, 110,000 different kinds of parts. If you have enormous numbers of corporations with hundreds of thousands of types of parts, in all kinds of different alloys and all kinds of association, what are you going to do in getting ready for World War III? How are you going to stockpile your resources? Quite clearly what had been a great failure in America during World Wars I and II was the thought that a single man could be a director of all war production. They took the smartest businessmen they had, but they always fell short of what they needed to do. You realize you are asking a human being to do more than he could possibly handle.

I spoke to you about a tool being an extension of a fundamental integral human function, but in designing the tool you could extend the limits of its capability. In inventing and proliferating the computer, done because after World War II science had the technological capability to do it, the human brain function was extended. Although the computers do nothing that a brain cannot do, they can do it longer and much more powerfully, much more swiftly, and can handle fantastic amounts of information and be preoccupied and hold this for you and file that and retrieve all of it very rapidly. That is all the computer is doing. It does nothing a brain cannot do, but it can do more of it than a brain can do. A computer is able to stay up all night, separating the pink from the yellow at speeds you can't possibly match under conditions of cold you can't support—you'd freeze to death.

The computer is about to take over what we call automation. People worry about automation although we've all been automated ourselves. You haven't the slightest idea what you are doing this minute with your dinner; you're not purposely sending the peas and rice to this or that gland to make hair; that's all automated. You haven't the slightest idea how you went from 7 pounds to 170; it was all automated. Nobody is saying: "I'm pushing each of my hairs out in various colors and sizes"—you don't even know why you have hair. It's all automated. We are about to have our computers take over the automation of the integrated tools that sustain you and me. Automation will take over those tools and it's going to make man utterly obsolete as a specialist. Man's going to be forced back to what he was born to be—a comprehensivist —to learn those generalized principles and to become master of his situation. This is what is coming up, if man is to make good on Earth—if we make good in time, if we catch on in time.

I've taken a great deal of your time; even so, there is still something else I would like to talk about. And I will talk about it just as fast as I know how. It relates to the young world and what is going on. Everybody is talking about "Be a man" etc. About war. We see how we got into war, all right. We have this working assumption that it has to be you or me and the Great State crowd saying that is so. I began to see in 1927— I had gotten out of the Navy in 1922, and I had gone into the building world and I found the building world five thousand years behind the technology we had at sea and in the sky. I found that no scientist had ever looked at the plumbing, and even now they haven't looked at it! I find that man is not doing anything about how to make himself a success. All technology is going into this great killing ring. I said: "I see that Malthus may be wrong. The whole rationale of war is the assumption that Malthus is right, that there is not enough for all of us." But what I was so impressed with, having come out of sea technology, was that we were doing so much more with so much less. I said Malthus didn't know that there was going to be any kind of refrigeration. He didn't know that the food he thought was going to rot in the fields could be preserved and could reach mouths way across the ocean. It was perfectly clear to me that we could do so much more with so much less. We just might be able to take care of everybody. Then

Malthus would be utterly wrong and we wouldn't
have to have a war.

We've all been working under the assumption
that man is destined to be a failure. I say man is
quite clearly like the hydrogen atom: designed to
be a success. He is a fantastic piece of design; it
is completely wrong to think he is meant to be a
failure. I assume he is supposed to be a success
and that he is supposed to use his mind to make
himself a success; and to understand things like
wealth, as I gave it to you a few minutes ago—to
understand those generalized principles and to
realize that when you employ them you aren't
"spending" anything of the universe. You are simply employing what the universe is—turning the
universe to your account. And that is what you are
meant to do in order to demonstrate man's success.

And so I said in 1927: I'm going to commit the
rest of my life to exploring the whole matter of doing more with less and seeing what would happen
if we took the kind of technology which had only
been applied in the sea and sky and applied it to
the land where people have been building all
those heavy buildings. In the years since then, I
have spoken to the architectural associations of
almost every country of the world, and in the different states and cities. I always ask the audience
if they will tell me what the building we're in
weighs. And I say: "Any hands?" No hands. I say

"Will you tell me just roughly within a hundred thousand tons?" No hands. So I say: "Give it to me roughly within a million tons." No hands. So quite clearly people, architects included, do not know what buildings weigh. If you don't know what a building weighs, you certainly don't know what its performance per pound is. If you don't know what it weighs, you are certainly not trying to do more with less. We try to be efficient in the design of the machinery inside our buildings, but the buildings themselves are certainly not thought of in this way.

It became perfectly clear to me long ago that, in our land economics, we could make fantastic strides; and that realization brought me into trying geodesic domes. I now have five thousand of them in fifty countries. Thousands of these domes are light enough, strong enough, sufficient enough to be delivered by air. They weigh only about three percent of the weight of a traditional building of equal span. They are also proof against earthquake and relatively fireproof (for a given amount of time, code determined). They bear up under arctic snowloads and hurricanes. They are doing these things at only three percent of the weight of the best known alternate conventional solutions for buildings. So I discovered there was fantastic room for improvement to be made for the living arts on dry land. My investigations made perfectly clear what upping performance per pound of employed resources can mean in economics. Incidentally, during the time between 1900 and today, in two-thirds of a century we have gone from less than 1 percent to more than 40 percent of humanity living at a high standard. In the same period the amount of resources per man has been continually decreasing, so we obviously did not accomplish that high standard of living as a result of our having more resources to exploit. It came only as fallout of the doing-more-with-less design philosophy.

Now it is quite clear that politics doesn't know anything about that. Current design standards will only take care of 44 percent of humanity, with the majority of people doomed to very short life and to great pain along the way. But there is nothing in politics except knowing how to do without or taking it from one and giving to the other. That is what the sociologists and politicians attempt to do. They still say it has to be just you *or* me. There's no real awareness among politicians anywhere around the world that there could be more-with-less to the point of making it possible for the world's available resources to take care of everybody—and at higher standards than anybody has dreamt of. But science now says that is perfectly possible. It has to do with something called "engineering efficiency"—the amount of work done by a machine out of the energy it consumes. A reciprocating engine, which you all have in your automobiles, is only 15 percent efficient. You have explosion at the top of the pistons and the energy is sent by connecting rod to crank shaft. So you send it down and the crank shaft sends it right back from where you sent it. It immediately contradicts you, and this is called a 180 degree restraint. And it is only 15 percent efficient; that's all you can get out of it. Now we have the explosion on this side of the piston instead of at its top. There is still a connecting rod but just a thick shaft and this system is called turbine. It has only a 90 degree restraint, and that is 30 percent efficient. I'm just giving you the approximate figures for this. Then we have the jet engine, which gets up to 60 percent efficiency. I've doubled each time, just removing those restraints. The overall efficiency of all the machinery man is using around the world today is only 4 percent. In engineering it is highly feasible to go to an overall 12; and if we do, we can take care of all humanity.

In talking about pure engineering feasibility, it is eminently clear to scientists that the job *can* be done. But they all also say you can't do it with any of the national boundary restrictions which "protect" the nations. Each one is thinking that it has to be his side which has the advantage. Everyone depends on protection. But to do the job man must have absolutely free intercourse and access to the distribution of resources found around the world. We have to deal with our space ship, Earth,

as a machine, which is what it is. You can't have a
machine where the U.S.S.R. is the spark plugs,
and the U.S.A. is the crank shaft, and the two
parts don't work together. Today's situation. And
we say: "How are you going to get out of this
mess?" Politics? No politician is allowed to yield to
another politician, and any political leader you
can get is going to be finally up against what
his military will tell him. The military will tell
him that the joint chiefs of staff of the United
States and the joint chiefs of staff in Russia, the
joint chiefs of staff of China, *et al.,* all operate
under John von Neumann's game theory. And
in game theory it's one side or the other. And
in this game theory of John von Neumann's, if one
side makes an altruistic move—it loses. If any political leader makes any kind of altruistic move or
statement, it is purely camouflage. If he made one
genuinely altruistic move, then he'd be saying:
"I'm choosing my side to lose," and no political
leader will do that. He may campaign otherwise
but he finally is going to be up against that military
saying: "You have the right to make the decision
that your side is to lose." He couldn't do that.

Logically, today's youth becomes exasperated
and asks: "Why can't we make the world work?"
All this negative nonsense is the consequence of
outworn, ignorant biases of old timers. I say let's
join forces and set things to rights. Parading in

multitudes, students demand that their political leaders take steps to bring about peace and plenty. The fallacy of this lies in their age-old and mistaken assumption that the problem is one of political reform. The fact is that the politicians are faced with a vacuum, and you can't reform a vacuum. The vacuum is the apparent world condition of not enough to go around, not enough for even a majority of mankind to survive more than half of its potential life span. It is again a you-or-me-to-the-death situation that leads from impasse to impasse to ultimate showdown by arms. Thus, more and more students around the world are learning of the new and surprising alternative to politics—the design-science revolution that alone can solve the problem.

Along with the 1965 Berkeley episodes and the myriad of civil disturbances which occurred in the United States as a result of the national reactionary pullback at the by-election polls in 1966, every college campus has had its quota of incidents. But in relation to this there are now new realizations. The students who graduated in June, 1966 were born and grew up under historically unprecedented conditions that are known by behavioral science research to have affected very seriously the intellectual and social development of humans. The university and college classes of 1966 were born as the first atomic bomb exploded over Hiroshima, killing and maiming vast numbers of civilians. The students of 1966 were the first human beings to be reared by the third parent—by television, whose voice and presence are seen and heard by children far more than those of the two blood parents. The real parents come home from the store, or office, or golf course, or hairdresser and say: "Wow! What a day! Let's have a beer," and sit down to small talk about local events—and the children slip off to hear the third parent brief them visually, ergo vividly, on the world-around news regarding the world's continual aches, pains, disasters, olympic triumphs, and all.

As the class of 1966 grew and developed from birth, they learned from the third parent about man's going across the North Pole under ice. In their fourteenth year, the Russian unmanned rocket photographed the far side of the moon and returned to earth. When they were fifteen, the U.S. bathyscaphe took man safely to photograph the bottom of the Pacific Ocean's deepest hole. In their sixteenth year, a Russian orbited earth in a rocket. As they reached seventeenth, the DNA genetic code for control of the design of all life was discovered. And then the class of 1966 at Berkeley shocked the world by saying that it felt no special loyalty to its families, its university, its state, or its nation. The youth of the class of 1966 were thought by most oldsters to be shockingly "immoral" and lacking in idealism. Not so. They are as idealistic and full of compassion as any child has ever been, but their loyalty is to all humanity. They are no longer the creatures of local, class, or race biases. They say: "Mankind can do anything it wants. Why don't our officials and families stop talking about their local biases and wasting wealth on warring—all because they assume that war is necessary simply because there does not seem to be enough to take care of even one-half of humanity's needs." Today's youth say: "Why not up the performance per unit of invested resources and thus make enough to go around?" And they're right.

Students can *learn* the following: that technical evolution has this fundamental behavior pattern. First, as I have explained to you, there is a scientific discovery of a generalized principle, which occurs as a subjective realization by experimentally probing man. Next comes objective employment of that principle in a special-case invention. Next, the invention is reduced to practice. This gives man an increased technical advantage over his physical environment. If successful as a tool of society, it is used in ever bigger, swifter, and everyday ways. For instance, it goes progressively from a little steel steamship to ever bigger fleets of constantly swifter, high-powered ocean giants.

There comes a time, however, when we discover other ways of doing the same task more economically. For instance, we discover that a 200-ton transoceanic jet airplane, considered on an annual round-trip frequency basis, can outperform the passenger-carrying capability of the 85,000 ton *Queen Elizabeth* or that a quarter-ton transoceanic communications relay satellite ourperforms 150,-000 tons of transoceanic cables. All the technical curves rise in tonnage and volumetric size to reach a giant peak, after which progressive miniaturization sets in. After that, a new and more economical art takes over which also goes through the same cycle of doing progressively more with less. First, by getting bigger and taking advantage, for instance, of the fact that doubling the length of a ship increases its wetted surface fourfold while increasing its payload volume eightfold. Inasmuch as the cost of driving progressively bigger ships through the water at a given speed increases in direct proportion to the increase in friction of the wetted surface, the eightfolding of payload volume gained with each fourfolding of wetted surface means twice as much profit for less effort each time the ship's length is doubled. This principle of advantage gain through geometrical-size increase holds true for ships of both air and water. Then doubling of length of sea-going ships finally runs into trouble; for instance, the ocean liner made more than a thousand feet long would have to span between two giant waves and would have to be doubled in size to do so. However, if doubled in size once more, she could no longer be accommodated by the great world canals, dry docks, and harbors.

At this point the miniaturization of doing more with less first ensues through substitution of an entirely new art. David's slingstone over Goliath's club operated from beyond reach of the giant. This overall and inexorable trending to do more with less is known sum totally as progressive ephemeralization. Ephemeralization trends toward an ultimate doing of everything with nothing at all— which is a trend of the omniweighable physical to be mastered by the omniweightless metaphysics of intellect. All the ballistic arts of man and men's warring to the death have followed this same fundamental evolutionary pattern of bigger, then smaller.

Assuming that there was not and never would be enough of the vital support resources to go around, and concluding that there must be repeating eventualities in wars to see which side could pursue its most favored theory of survival under fundamental inadequacies, humanity has continually done more killing with less human effort at greater and greater distances and at ever higher speeds with ever increasing accuracy. Humanity's killing capability has gone from a thrown stone to a spear to a sling to a bow and arrow to a pistol, a musket, a cannon, and so on to the great weapons-carrying battleships. Then suddenly a little two-ton torpedo-carrying airplane sank a 45,000-ton battleship, and then the 2,000 miles-per-hour airplane was out-performed by the 16,000 miles-per-hour atom-bomb-carrying rocket, a miniscule weight in comparison to the bomb-carrying plane. If world-warring persists as a consequence of the concept of survival only of the fittest minority, there will come the virtually weightless death-rays operating at 700-million miles per hour. At the present point of history, the uranium bomb has been recently displaced by the hydrogen bomb until it was dis-covered that if either side used that new greatest weapon, both sides and the rest of humanity would perish. Therefore, the biggest weapons could not be used, nor could the equally large and mutually destructive biological or chemical gas warfaring. Then both sides discovered that killing of the enemy's people was not their objective. Killing the enemy's *ideology* is the objective. Killing the enemy's people brings sympathy and support for the enemy from the rest of the world, and gaining the good opinion and support of the rest of the world is one of the new world's war aims.

And now? Both sides have started to explore the waging of more war with lesser, more limited killings, but more politically and economically de-vastating techniques. Just as ephemeralization (employing ever more miniscule instruments) took technology out of the limited ranges of the human senses into the vast and invisible ranges of the electromagnetic spectrum, so too has major warfaring almost disappeared from the visible contacts of human soldiery and entered into the realm of invisible psychology. In the new invisible miniaturization phase of major world warring, both sides carry on an attention-focusing guerrilla warfare, as now in Vietnam, while making their most powerful attacks through subversion, vandalism, or skillful agitation of any and all possible areas of discontent within the formally assumed enemy's home economics.

In carrying on this new and unfamiliar world warring, they don't have to send ideological proselytizers to persuade the people of the other side to abandon their home country's political systems and adopt that of their former enemy. Instead they can readily involve, induce, and persuade individuals of the other side to look for discontent wherever it manifests itself and thereafter to amplify that condition by whatever psychological means until the situation erupts in public demonstrations etc. The idea is to make a mess of the other's economy and thereby discredit his socio-political system in the eyes of the rest of the world and to destroy the enemy people's confidence in its own system. Because the active operators are most often engaged on the basis of just gratifying their own personal discontent, they are most often unaware that they are acting as agents. Because almost everyone has at least one discontent, a single well-trained, conscious agent can evoke the effective but unwitting agency of hundreds of other discontents, promoters, and joiners. As a consequence of this new invisible phase of world war trending, a most paradoxical condition exists wherein the highly idealistic youth of college age, convinced that they are demonstrating against war, are in fact the front line soldiers operating as unwitting shock troops while the conventionally recognized soldiers, engaged in visible war-zone warfare either of ambush or open battle, are carrying on only a secondary, albeit often mortally fatal, decoy operation.

This invisible world-around warring to destroy the enemy's economy wherever it is operative, above all by demonstrating its homeland weaknesses and vulnerabilities to the rest of the world and thus hopefully destroying the confidence of the enemy people in themselves, is far more devastating than a physical death ray could be; for it does everything with nothing. Furthermore, it operates as news that moves around the earth by electromagnetic waves operating at 700-million miles per hour. At the moment, the highly controlled political state has a great defensive advantage over the open, freedom-nurturing states by virtue of the former's controlled news, for it is the omniexcitable news in the free countries which is primarily exploited to publish, spread, and thus create a chain reaction of dismay through the guaranteed publishing of any and all of their organized-discontent activities.

While all the foregoing curves of rising and falling in the technical evolution of weaponry have taken place, there has also occurred, all unnoticed to the parties of the warfaring, a vast fallout from the defense technology into the domestic technology of ephemeralization's doing ever more with ever less. As I remarked, within two-thirds of a century this unnoticed and inadvertent fallout has converted forty-plus percent of total humanity from havenotness to a high standard of living-haveness and made clear that the only way all humanity may be elevated to such an advantage is by further acceleration of this technological revolution.

It becomes evident, then, that youth's world-around clamor for peace can only be realized through technological revolution, which will do so much more with so much less per each function as ultimately to produce enough to support all humanity. It is also clear that such a task can *only* be accomplished by this technological design revolution. As many who have become involved in the new invisible warfaring discover that their aim can only be attained through this design revolution, all the young world-around idealists will have to face the question of whether they prefer to keep on agitating simply because they have come to enjoy a sense of power and importance by doing so, or whether they really are dedicated to the earliest possible attainment of economic and physical success for all humanity and thereby realistically to eliminate war.

If the desire for the elimination of war is what they are most moved by, they will have to shift their effort from mere political agitation to participation in the design science revolution. The latter course involves the development of ever self-regenerating and improving scientific and technical competence, and that in turn means the individual must plunge earnestly and dedicatedly into self-development by the resources of an educational system designed to develop the inherent comprehensivity of humanity.

OCTOBER, 1968

Engineers and the Nation's Future

ERIC A. WALKER

❦

It is an honor and a pleasure to be a speaker for the distinguished Franklin Lectures in the Sciences and Humanities. The subject that I would like to talk to you about is one that I know you'll be hearing a lot about in the near future. More and more the question keeps cropping up—what are the responsibilities of the engineering and science communities in the future development of the nation? What are the responsibilities of science and engineering to humanity? And in which direction should we be moving?

From the engineering point of view, there are some who believe that the engineering profession should stick strictly to the technical end of the business. There are others, however, who believe that engineering must broaden its responsibilities.

Yet there is no agreement on how this broadening should be done, or through which instruments.

In spite of the engineering developments that have reshaped the modern world, there has often been a tendency in the popular mind to confuse the goals and purposes of the scientists on the one hand with those of the engineer on the other. Yet the distinction is clear enough.

In basic terms, the job of the scientist is to inquire into the workings of nature and to seek the understanding of them—to accumulate scientific information for its own sake.

The task of the engineer, however, is to use this information in the most practical and effective way possible, to create the devices and systems that are needed for the comfort, convenience, and progress of modern man.

Developments of the past several decades, however, have somewhat altered this basic distinction between science and engineering. The rapid and extensive growth of research, in industry, in educational institutions, and within the government itself, has tended to pull the scientist and the engineer closer together, and blur the differences in their separate approaches to the requirements of modern life. The engineer, in his design of new and sophisticated devices, has become increasingly dependent upon the newly-found knowledge of the scientist, and does more research himself. And the scientist himself has frequently found it necessary to work hand-in-hand with the engineer and at times be a designer and engineer.

So today, in the public's mind, there seems to be no clear-cut distinction between the activities of the scientist and those of the engineer. Yet the distinction does exist.

In his book, "Two Cultures and the Scientific Revolution," C. P. Snow pointed out that a great gulf exists between this science-engineering complex on the one hand, and the rest of the population—particularly, he says, the literary intellectuals —on the other. Snow blames this gulf on the lack of communication between the two groups and he says that it well could be fatal to the Western world.

Yet, the gulf is deeper, broader, and somewhat different from that, and the real problem is not in communications as such. The real gulf today, I believe, lies between what science and engineering are capable of doing for mankind on the one hand, and what the average citizen is getting as a result of all this knowledge, on the other.

There was a time, up until a few decades ago, when we were a nation of practical doers who could put together machines and do almost anything. We developed the telegraph, the telephone, the sewing machine, and the cotton gin. Men like Edison came along and provided a score of practical inventions for this nation and for the world. Almost anything engineers did to harness nature then was considered good. The engineer was the builder of the highways, bridges, skyscrapers, and the designer of the industrial machinery and the processes that made our factories grow. And at first, if the highways got a little crowded, or the fumes from the factory darkened the skies, or if the tightly packed skyscrapers crowded too many people together in one spot—well, that was considered the necessary price of progress.

During those years, we did almost nothing about pure science. We believed and demonstrated that necessity was the mother of invention. We knew how to make good Kentucky rifles before we knew anything about the science of metallurgy. And steam engines worked successfully and provided power before we understood the laws of thermodynamics. Yet as a result of our inventiveness, our ingenuity, and our practical know-how, we built up an economic base that enabled us to support pure science, art, music, and literature.

But then along came World War II, and men recognized that the war would be won and our nation would survive only by the development of weapons and systems not yet in existence. We began to mobilize our scientific and technical resources on a scale never before witnessed.

Our success during the war in the large-scale use of newly found scientific knowledge in the production of military weapons—especially the atom bomb —taught us several important lessons. It not only emphasized the importance of the essential link between discovery and application, but it made us conscious of our neglect, as a nation, of basic research. And most importantly, it provided us with a model of what could be accomplished through an organized process of research, development, pilot production, and final product.

At the end of the war, it was apparent that, in many areas, our wartime achievements had direct application to peacetime goals, and it seemed evident that, in some respects at least, a continuation of the methods and practices which had brought us military success might be desirable in peacetime. And since it was also evident that a great deal of the success in the war had been the result of our own scientific discoveries, it seemed neither desirable nor possible for us to depend, as we had largely done before the war, upon European sources for basic scientific information. If the United States was to maintain its technological superiority and stay ahead of the rest of the world, it seemed obvious that we must not only continue to nourish and use science but that wide-scale scientific research should be supported as a national policy.

The result, of course, was that the government, which had been the major supporter of science during the war, continued in the business of providing funds and personnel for scientific research. Support was given for research in the semi-private and private sectors of the economy by giving research contracts to industry and to universities and other non-profit organizations.

In short, basic scientific research came to be accepted as an essential national activity, and our political leaders, our industrial leaders, and indeed the general public itself became convinced of its importance as a basis for the continued economic progress and general well-being of the nation. And, as Americans usually do, we jumped in with both feet. Within a few years our support for basic science exceeded that of all the rest of the world put together. And the number of papers and publications in pure science rose astronomically, as did the number of Nobel Prize winners. Indeed, so assiduously did we follow the path of pure science that during the last 18 years we have won 40 Nobel Prizes in the science fields alone—more than any other single nation. And in 1968, the United States won all the Nobel Prizes in the fields of physics, chemistry, medicine, and physiology.

Now the consequences of this attitude toward research have been widespread. There is no doubt that our organized and well-supported research activity has kept America in the forefront of modern science. And it is apparent that some of our industries have learned to integrate research and development laboratories into their systems—to their own benefit and that of the customers who use their products.

It is true that, in some areas, our industrial enterprise has profited from the "spin-off" of government-sponsored activity. But perhaps the most significant consequence of this large-scale government support of research has been the new opportunities and challenges that have been opened up and that have prompted us to take a more careful look at the whole complex process by which new scientific knowledge can be converted into useful goods and services.

Until a few years ago, we seem to have made the assumption that so long as we provided enough funds for basic research, the new knowledge we discovered would almost automatically be translated into products and systems and services that would enrich our lives and create general prosperity. And indeed there is evidence that in some instances this sort of transfer occurs quickly. Yet in the past few years, we have had reason to question how widespread this process of transfer really is. Many of our Congressmen and other public officials have begun to wonder whether the fantastic sums of public money that are being poured into basic research are really paying off in terms of practical progress. In many instances it would appear that knowledge is accumulating at such a rate and to an extent that it cannot possibly be used effectively without a more conscious effort to put it to practical use for the good of humanity.

We are filling our libraries with an almost unbelievable amount of new knowledge, and we ask ourselves what practical use can be made of all these facts, theories, and discoveries. Is the growth of our funding of basic research disproportionate to the growth of our gross national product? Can we continue to give an ever increasing share of our GNP to science? If so, who gets less—welfare, health care, highways, or old age pensions? Should we not examine more critically the whole process of innovation and invention, the means by which basic knowledge is actually applied to practical use? Have we failed to give proper attention to this vital step in the process?

The trouble is that, while we have expended a good deal of money on pure science, we have not done enough on the engineering end of the problem for our people. Now once again Americans are beginning to ask the question: "Of what value is pure science to me?"

It is my belief that the average citizen in America today looks around him and is not satisfied with what science and engineering have given him. Let me rephrase that and say that the public is not satisfied mainly because there are many things that could be done for the citizen which are not being done by the scientists and engineers who are using public money. Today we are witnessing a great deterioration in the quality of our lives, caused principally, I believe, because of this situation. For example, we have gone to the moon, and here on earth we have very fine automobiles, very fine airplanes, and in many places very fine highways. But the average citizen still can't get from one place to another rapidly and safely.

How do you think the average motorist feels when he hears that our space vehicles can travel 25,000 miles per hour on the way to the moon, when he must spend the same hour in bumper to bumper traffic getting between his job and his home a few miles away? Programmed highways have been on the drawing boards for years, but no one has done anything about building one. There is no dignity left in trying to get from say New York to Washington, or from University Park, Pennsylvania to Auburn, Alabama by present methods. There is no comfort—in fact it's an indecent struggle.

Our travel methods, which are now concentrated mainly in travel by air and automobile, are obviously going to decline still further as our ground transportation from airport to city gets more complex, more dirty, more vulgar, and more uncivilized. The airports themselves have become overloaded, garish, trashy, littered, and noisy. A recent issue of *Saturday Review* defined an air traveler as a man who spends 60 per cent of his time in traffic jams getting to the airport and 40 per cent in traffic jams in the air.

Alan S. Boyd, former Secretary of Transportation, said recently that the problem of sufficient airport access capacity is plaguing every major airport in the world. For example, the line of cars waiting to get to Chicago's O'Hare Airport last Thanksgiving, he said, stretched five miles. The Los Angeles International Airport had to go on the air every hour during the day prior to last Christmas to warn of the parking-space shortage. Air traffic controllers trying to get to work at Miami International were stalled in traffic for two and a half hours just trying to get from the entrance of the airport to the terminal.

If the access roads are crowded, it is clear that the airport runways and air corridors will become even more crowded in the years ahead if something isn't done. Airlines are receiving on the average one new jet a day. General aviation adds eighty-five new planes a week to the airways. Thus we can expect a doubling of takeoffs and landings at FAA controlled airports within five years and a quadrupling by 1980. Last year, airlines carried more than 150 million passengers, and companies claim they are adding new passengers at the rate of 40,000 a day. If these figures are accurate and the trend continues, more than one and a half million passengers will climb aboard airliners each day in 1980.

Ground transportation by train has become almost torture, and no one in America seems to be doing very much to bring it back to its former state of respect. Indeed, Americans are becoming envious of the solutions the Japanese and the Canadians apparently have found for their highspeed rail transportation and they wonder why we cannot do the same. It hardly seems possible that only a hundred years ago this May, Leland Stanford drove the last spike to complete the transcontinental railroad that was supposed to be the beginning of a new era for passenger travel across country. Now, after a century of railroading, the long-haul passenger business is almost bankrupt. According to a recent issue of *Saturday Review,* it is quite likely that there are fewer passengers riding the nation's trains today than in 1860. The paradox is that while we have more than 200,000 miles of railroad track in the forty-eight contiguous states—which is more than any other nation—two-thirds of that track lies unused and rusting. Six years ago, Senator Claiborne Pell of Rhode Island urged a study of railroad potential in 22 heavily populated, heavily traveled corridors. It was found that modern passenger trains could cut airway and highway congestion significantly between cities 150 and 350 miles apart. Yet virtually nothing is being done. It has been estimated that a single railroad track can transport as many passengers per hour as a twenty-lane expressway. And modern high-speed trains, running on electricity and using existing rights-of-way, would cut our air pollution, thin our traffic jams, and prevent unnecessary highway projects from chopping up the heart of our cities and countryside.

The problem of pollution—of the air, the land, and our streams—is getting more severe each year, and solutions that are being attempted are obviously far from adequate. Our garbage is not properly disposed of, old automobiles are left lying around everywhere, and beer cans and trash abound in our parks and along our highways. Our sewage plants are overloaded and primitive, and very little experimentation is going on with new systems, while our streams are polluted with trash, sewage, chemicals, and hot water.

Chauncey Starr, dean of engineering at UCLA, says in a recent publication that many of our environmental pollution problems have presently known engineering solutions—but the problems of economic readjustment, political jurisdiction, and social behavior loom as very large obstacles. If we continue on the current path, he says, it will take many decades to put into practice the technical solutions we know today. As a specific illustration, the pollution of our water resources is completely avoidable by engineering systems now available; but, in fact, interest in making the economic and political adjustments to apply these techniques is very limited. In most cases town fathers just don't want to take the risk of trying new and expensive systems. And I wouldn't either if my reelection hung on the failure of an engineering experiment. It has been facetiously suggested that, as a means of motivating people, every community and industry should be required to place its drinking water intake downstream from its sewage discharges.

We will soon spend millions to probe the atmosphere of Venus and Mars, while the air here on earth remains polluted with dust and heat with which we cannot cope. Indeed it may be a good thing that ships from other planets are not sampling our atmosphere—the conclusion might well be that life cannot possibly exist on earth.

While we have developed an efficient voice transportation system, and can talk to almost anyone all over the country, our delivery systems for written messages, food supplies, fuel supplies, packages and such is woefully inadequate. Certainly, new and better methods of making deliveries—such as the use of pneumatic tubes for letters and parcels, which have been used for years—must be rediscovered and developed.

Our educational system seems so cluttered that we have forgotten that the purpose of an educational system is to give everybody as much education as he wants and can use. But now we seem determined to give everybody the same kind of education regardless of whether he is ready for it or can use it. Our educational system seems to have become completely disconnected from what society needs. We are educating people who cannot make use of their education, and so we have thousands of untrained unemployed with at least an equal number of jobs unfilled. Obviously a re-study of the whole educational system, to make it useful for people and society, is again needed.

Our governmental systems have never seemed so inadequate. We are saddled with systems like school boards, school districts, town meetings, borough councils, district government, and county government, many of which overlap; while at the same time there is little or no clear definition of what the states are supposed to do and what is reserved for the federal government.

To support all this we have an amazingly complicated taxation system which taxes things more than once, which taxes more things out of proportion to their usefulness and taxes inequitably between the rich and the poor. The whole governmental system may be creaking toward a collapse of its own weight, unless something is done soon.

In the field of medicine we are capable of producing numerous devices for the benefit of patients —yet many of these developments never get to the marketplace simply because there is no profit in producing them. For example, earlier this year a young Marine corporal was fitted with a newly developed electronic arm at the Temple University Health Science Center in Philadelphia. The new type arm responds to brain signals which are picked up by way of probes in the shoulder. The arm, which can be flexed at the elbow, swung from the shoulder, and rotated at the wrist, is described as "fantastic" by both its user and those who witnessed its use. Yet it is likely that such a device will never be produced in any sufficient quantity because of the heavy cost of production and the little or no profit involved.

Finally, our cities continue to exist with over-crowding, ghetto living, deteriorating buildings that are a haven for rats, lack of open space, and conditions so miserable for some of our citizens that both mind and body are withered. What values have we set for ourselves as a nation when some men must live in such primitive conditions while others cruise the universe in germ-free, sterile space cabins.

It is only fair to say, of course, that there is evidence that we have begun to recognize the housing challenge, at least in some quarters. For example, the National Academy of Engineering is talking about a proposal put together some time ago by the President's Office of Science and Technology for an Interagency Family Housing Demonstration Program. This would leap over local codes, union rules, and antiquated assembly processes to build good houses inexpensively.

Recognizing that real innovation in the construction of housing units is technologically possible and highly desirable, but that development of new techniques has been hampered by the fragmentation of the industry, code constraints, rigid labor practices, and government apathy, the OST proposed an extensive project, to be undertaken jointly by the Department of Housing and Urban Development, and the Department of Defense. The idea was to start from scratch, so to speak, by securing a large area outside the jurisdiction of local building codes or other restrictions, and attack the problem of family housing in much the same way that a large and complicated weapons system is attacked, through a program advancing from small-scale field experimentation and evaluation to prototypes, to large-scale procurement for demonstration purposes. Every possible use is to be made of new techniques and innovations. It is expected that by using government construction funds to demonstrate the practicality of advanced building systems, the stage could be set for substantial improvement in low-income housing nationally. Projects of this sort, I think, are badly needed. For it is clear to me that if improvements don't come in all these situations we will reach a time when people will demand that something be done. And after all, it is the average citizen who is paying the bill in this country.

It is my feeling that these problems, taken together, are as severe as they were when we were menaced by enemies during the first and second World Wars. We all know that during those wars, the nation's and the people's entire energies were devoted to overcoming our problems. We turned our entire attention to the practical aspects of science and engineering to get something done—something that was needed immediately in the face of clear and present danger. We mobilized all our resources. I believe that we are again in the middle of a crisis—a clear and present danger—although many of us don't recognize it as that yet.

Perhaps what must be done again is that the whole country should be mobilized to solve these national problems—government, industry, the public, pure scientists, applied scientists, engineers, and businessmen. Perhaps we could have a "call to arms" in which the Federal and State governments recognize that the solution to these public problems is important and crucial. Perhaps with the end of the Vietnam War we can turn our attention—our whole attention and not partial attention—to the solution of such problems. Perhaps there could be a four-year period in which the whole country "wars" on the deterioration of the quality of our life. This would take mobilization of all our efforts, from the highest level on down, including the Department of Defense, the Space Agency, the National Science Foundation, the National Academy of Engineering, and all our universities.

What, you may ask, will we be doing about basic research while we have our energies turned toward practical problems?

Basic research did not suffer permanently when we devoted all our energies to the practical problems of two world wars. And I think that history has proven that as soon as any war is over we have redirected our attention to catch up on all the basic research which we might have done and did not do. We have been hearing a great deal recently from scientists about the need for more support for basic research. There has been a great deal of talk about the lack of support by the federal government in basic research and even statements to the fact that our superiority in science is going to fade away unless something is done about it immediately. Really, I put very little stock in such comments. People—and this country as well—get somewhere only by doing something that is difficult to do. That is why we stretch our muscles and that is why we train and exercise and exert ourselves. I suspect that there would be nothing wrong with having a squeeze on basic research once in a while—if only to sharpen our wits and increase our efficiency. Anyway, I think it's a bit difficult to claim that we are losing our superiority in basic science when in the past year we have won all the Nobel Prizes there are in science.

There is no doubt in my mind that if we turn our attention now to practical problems and are willing to wage a war against the deterioration in the quality of our lives—even for as short a period as four years—the advance we could achieve for humanity would be phenomenal. And it would set us apart as a nation for all to follow—a nation which is willing to seriously approach the problems of its citizens and find the solutions for them. To do so would not be a difficult task when one considers that approximately ninety per cent of all the scientists and engineers who ever lived are alive today.

Certainly a large share of the blame for our slowness to act on these national problems must be laid to technology itself—to the engineer who has traditionally confined his interests all too narrowly to his technical specialty, and who is only beginning to take his proper place in the mainstream of social activity. It seems to me that, more than any other group, the engineering profession must accept this new responsibility wholeheartedly.

The world of the engineer can no longer be limited to the concerns of business and industry, or even to the traditional requirements in the field of public works. Along with the rest of society, the engineer is faced with the task of finding solutions to these pressing problems of modern life—problems which lie in the public sector of our economy. Basically, many of these problems are engineering problems. To a large extent, their ultimate solutions will depend upon the willingness and ability of the engineering community to provide society with the kind of help and advice that is needed to solve them.

Engineering must, and is, more and more recognizing the importance of the social sciences, the humanities, and the communication skills in the undergraduate programs. It is evident that the engineer of the future will be called upon more and more to play an increasingly active role in the solution of complex social problems. He will have to cope not only with the physical forces, as in the past, but with biological, social, and political forces. As a consequence, engineering education in the years ahead—as well as science education—will have to impart a thorough knowledge of the many non-technical aspects of modern life. And the humanities, too, must begin to learn more and more about the professions of science and engineering, and must learn to work more closely with their colleagues in these fields.

Just as our government has financed big science, it must now finance big engineering. But the engineers must prove that they are able to take government money to solve the people's problems and give them what they need to be productive, efficient, and contented citizens. To make a start in solving these national problems would bring us a great deal more prestige as a nation—prestige that we have been losing for the past several years.

Lincoln reminded us that a house divided against itself cannot long stand. So too, a nation that devotes a great deal of its energies and resources to pure science without an equal return in practical benefits for the citizens who are paying the bill, cannot hope to have the support of its citizens. We must not forget, as we reach out into the universe, that this government was founded to "insure domestic tranquillity" and to "promote the general welfare"—right here on earth.

APRIL, 1969

Toward a Working Partnership of the Sciences and Humanities

JAMES R. KILLIAN, JR.

৩৯৩

I COUNT IT A PRIVILEGE to participate in Auburn's Franklin Lectures in the Sciences and Humanities. My appearance here allows me to share in your tribute to John Leonard Franklin and to add my own appreciation of his rare qualities as an inventor and humanist. This lectureship also provides me with an opportunity to discuss a subject that has long been in the foreground of my thoughts.

Inevitably lectures dealing with the sciences and the humanities must run the risk of being merely footnotes to the great debate that Matthew Arnold, Bishop Wilberforce, and Thomas Huxley pursued with such vigor and vehemence, and that Sir Charles Snow and Frank Leavis have so recently updated—or backdated! What I say to you does not avoid echoes of that classic controversy, but I do hope also to move beyond their locus of battle and in the end to suggest out of my personal experience some down-to-earth but formidable examples of current issues, the resolution of which can be facilitated by a working partnership of the sciences and humanities, whatever may be their differences in mode and outlook. In fact, our society is confronted with a host of problems that in my view can best be solved by activists from the sciences, the social sciences, and the humanities together contributing out of their specialized insights to the common account. Through their joint efforts in the public arena may lie our best hope for providing a program for a better society—better both for the lonely crowd and for the lonely human being.

Implicit in all that I say in this lecture is a plea that more humanists, scientists, and social scientists re-examine their relationships to society and descend from their ivory towers to engage in the grubby but vital social action that is required to advance the quality of our society. Both the humanities and the sciences have lost prestige and are in trouble today. The humanities are still too much afflicted by what George Santayana called the genteel tradition. As some of my colleagues in the humanities put it recently in an internal memorandum, "we share the suspicion that a severe kind of professionalism and a hardening of archaic 19th century attitudes threaten the teaching of the humanities in the U.S. with a complacent and deadly kind of Mandarinism."

The sciences are also in trouble because they are associated in the minds of many, not so much with their socially constructive effects as with terrifying military technology and with the degradation of our environment through misapplied technology.

Is it not possible that closer couplings between the sciences and the humanities may help both?

In the spirit of these introductory observations, let me now turn to the Huxley-Arnold-Snow tradition, pipe some notes on my penny whistle, and review recent comments by informed observers.

I believe strongly that the future vigor and welfare of our society require that our science and technology flourish, but I believe with equal conviction that the humanities and arts must flourish too, and that our ultimate aim in learning and living should be to avoid detrimental conflicts and to achieve a confluence of these two domains. In a very deep sense they are interdependent, and they spring from the same act of imagination.

In his posthumously published Pegram Lectures, André Maurois recounts an anecdote told to him by the poet Saint-John Perse. Once while he was living in Washington, Einstein called him from Princeton and asked him to come to see him. "I have a question to ask you," said Einstein. Saint-John Perse did visit Einstein, and the great physicist put to him the question: "How does the poet work? How does the idea of a poem come to him? How does this idea grow? Saint-John Perse described the vast part played by intuition and by the subconscious. Einstein seemed delighted: "But it's the same thing for the man of science," he said. "The mechanics of discovery are neither logical nor intellectual. It is a sudden illumination, almost a rapture. Later, to be sure, intelligence, analysis, and experiments confirm (or invalidate) the intuition. But initially there is a great forward leap of the imagination."

It is the humanistic responsibility of our colleges and universities to stress this kinship, indeed the unity, of all creative work and to ease the vested interests and snobberies which all too often appear among learned men.

We need to remind ourselves of the subtle couplings interconnecting the sciences, the social sciences, and the humanities. We need to remember how the great humanists of Greece, of the Middle Ages, and of the Renaissance helped to create an intellectual and spiritual environment and attitude benign to the development of modern science. Some of the great men of religion made their contribution. St. Francis of Assisi led men to seek spiritual elevation in nature itself; Roger Bacon, the friar, stressed the study of nature as another way to perceive God; Peter Abelard foreshadowed the method of science when he wrote: "By doubting we are led to inquire, and by inquiring to perceive truth." Thus nature gained importance as a domain for study, and thus science came to be encouraged. As Crane Brinton observed in *Ideas and Men*, "science needed not merely an interest in material things; it needed the intellectual apparatus to devise the incredibly complex ordering of things we call science; it needed above all the long training in the use of reason afforded by the Greek and medieval philosophy and theology our innocent logical positivists scorn."

Humanism is no less important today as an ally of science in the great coalition, the unity of learning we seek. The humanist is one of the principal architects and custodians of the benign environment which science requires for its success. The aesthetic sensitivities the great humanist cultivates or makes us aware of, the perspectives of history he reveals, and the questions about the future he insists on asking, the "vision of greatness" and the "study of perfection" he brings before us, his search for the moral and the first-rate in living, the eternal questions he asks—all these activities help to create the conditions and the outlook which science requires to flourish and men require for fulfillment.

We need also to remember how science has broken shackles of ignorance and superstition, given new leads in the social sciences, profoundly influenced and enriched the philosophy and the understanding of men, and thereby given a new depth and reach to humanism. Charles Frankel has called science "an example par excellence of a liberal art—a deliberate, selective reordering of experience, which releases men from the narrowness and urgency of their routine affairs . . . and makes it possible for their commerce with the world to have scope, order, and systematic consequences."

In recalling these special characteristics and interrelationships of science and the humanities, I do not minimize the continuing gap between them. Several years ago the American Academy of Arts and Sciences sponsored a conference on "Science and Culture," and in the issue of *Daedalus* devoted to the conference, Gerald Holton reported as follows:

. . . this very diverse group of about thirty-five men and women, including scientists, scholars in the humanities, creative artists, social scientists, and administrators, found fairly quickly one area of substantial agreement. It was the feeling that the relationship between the sciences and the humanities may well become considerably more strained in the immediate future. This estimate did not neglect the many new and old areas of mutual help nor the fact that there has always been some background noise of mutual invective. Here we are speaking of something new. As one concerned scientist expressed it, "we may not have seen anything yet of the row that is really going to develop." For example, one may expect drastic advances in the possibilities of increasing control over the human environment as well as over psychological and physiological functions (as by the action of drugs and the transplantation of organs); and this will have "a deep effect on what it is to be a human being." A sociologist agreed completely: "I think that the development of the in-between sphere (where both the sciences and the humanities have claims) is going to force many, many fights; they have been developing rapidly, and we have seen only the barest beginning of what is coming."

Despite this foreboding about territorial aggression between the two domains, I still think it important to stress the interdependence of the two fields and of trends toward convergence and unitary vision.

I have been speaking mainly of science and the humanities, but I would not neglect engineering nor applied science and the humanities. Curiously the tendency to give applied science a lower rank in the intellectual pecking order may have been revived by certain snobberies in the humanities. In an article in *Encounter* in 1965, Peter B. Medawar, Director of London's National Institute for Medical Research, made the interesting point that our current reverence for pure science derives from the "literary propaganda of the romantic revival." Said he in that article:

If our reverence for Pure Science is a rather parochial thing, a by-product of literary propaganda of the ro-

mantic revival; if no case can be made for it on philo-
sophic grounds; if purity is not part of a scientist's own
valuation of science; then why on earth do we think so
highly of it? It is, I think, our humanist brethren who
have taught us to believe that while pure science is a
genteel and even creditable activity for scientists and
universities, applied science, with all of its horrid con-
notations of trade, has no place on the campus; for only
the purest of pure science can give countenance to research in the humanities . . .

This invidious distinction between pure and applied science is akin to the classical distinction
between thought and practice—mind and hand—
the attitude, still to be found in some societies,
that spurns manual work as unfit for intellectuals.

Be that as it may, I wish to reiterate a view that
I have often stated about the widening role of the
engineer and the potentially close relationship between the humanist and the engineer. The engineer's professional responsibility has never been
so central to our society as it is today. I speak
primarily of the engineer who, in Ashby's phrase,
"views technology as inseparable from men and
communities." I speak of the engineer who has
achieved a mastery of his specialty but who, in
addition, has the capacity and motivation to use
and shape technology as a powerful humanistic
instrument for enchancing the quality of our society as well as its material advance, for helping
to solve the social problems of our time, and for

directing technology toward aesthetic and moral objectives. When working in close harmony with humanists, the engineer today occupies this position of great social responsibility. He occupies a unique vantage point for harnessing both science and the humanities for coping with some of the most urgent problems of our time—the crisis in transportation, the maintenance of a benign environment, the humane use of computer technology, preserving the beauty and benignity of our land.

We must, of course, recognize the importance of those engineers—the great specialists—who limit themselves to dedicated, creative technical work, and we honor them no less by stressing the need for humanist-engineers who accept the more comprehensive responsibility now so important to our society.

One of my colleagues, Professor Jay Forrester, has spoken of this urgently needed new engineer as an "enterprise engineer" or a "socio-technical systems engineer," and he believes that a "tenfold increase in the yield of enterprise engineer caliber of men calls for an entirely different kind of educational institution . . . that focuses on the gap in the upper elite sector of engineering practice."

Both the schools and the engineering profession itself must turn their attention toward creating the engineer who can provide the kind of professional leadership I have sought to describe. I call again for a major effort in our schools and in our professional societies to create the context out of which this kind of engineer can emerge.

The historian, Professor Lynn White, Jr., has suggested that engineers can help shape a new humanism. "Engineers are the chief revolutionaries of our time." he says.

Their implicit ideology is a compound of compassion for those suffering from physical want, combined with a Promethean rebellion against all bonds, even bonds to this planet. Engineers are arch-enemies of all who, because of their fortunate position, resist the surge of the mass of mankind toward a new order of plenty, of mobility, and of personal freedom. Within the societies which have consolidated about the Marxist and the Western democratic revolutions, engineers' activities are the chief threat to surviving privilege.

Without deliberate intent, but by the nature of their activity, engineers have largely destroyed the contemporary validity of the older aristocratic humanism which was a cultural weapon in the hands of the ruling class. When engineers in greater numbers come to know explicitly what they are doing, when they recognize their dedication, they can join with alert humanists to shape a new humanism which will speak for and to a global democratic culture.

Not only are there many intersections between the humanities and the sciences and engineering, but also between the arts and science. Advances in science have clearly given new dimensions to art. Leonardo the artist, as well as Leonardo the engineer, was a truth-seeker, and the Renaissance came to be a time when art and science most nearly converged—at least in spirit.

Whether the progress of science is constantly shaped to some degree by the larger cultural movements is more uncertain and more difficult to argue. Yet I remember well a conversation I had some forty years ago with the late great mathematician Norbert Wiener, who expressed to me his own conviction that *mathematics,* at least, "has been an active participant in the larger aesthetic movements." Later in 1930, Wiener set these ideas down in an article on "Mathematics and Art" in *The Technology Review.* He essayed to show how mathematics is a fine art as close to that of music, of literature, of painting as these are one to another and that it has shared in the characteristic style of the philosophy and aesthetics and general culture that differentiates, more or less, one period from another in the history of Western civilization.

As an example of the Wiener argument let me quote his comments on the transition from the Romantic period in mathematics to the present. "The romantic period," he says,

. . . carries us well towards the later years of the Nineteenth Century. The period of self-satisfaction in mathematics and in physics which ensued thereon, the period in which the physicist's ideal was the addition of another decimal place to already established constants and in which many a mathematician envisages the future as an absolutely traditional pursuit of lines of research already mapped out, is but the mirror of the Philistinism which has architecturally so disfigured Europe and America, the era of the red plush sofa. The present epoch both in the mathematical disciplines and in the arts represents a revolt against this Philistinism. The spirit underlying both revolts may be regarded as a development of romanticism. The romantic artist struck out on a line of his own in revolt against the rigidity of the Eighteenth Century. The artist of the present also regards it as his privilege to experiment and to adopt totally new methods; but, and this is important, without the act of assent that marks the true romanticist. The romanticist said, "I believe in this new art, as against the vitiated tradition." The modernist says, "This idea looks interesting to me. Let me see where it leads me, even though I may give it no ultimate approval." . . . Einstein developed his full gravitational theory in the beginning as a *tour de force*, as a possibility, interesting whether true or false. That it was ultimately to be verified reflects enormous credit on his intuition, but even unverified, it already existed as a mathematical essence, and this essence, this construction, parallels closely the goal of the effort of the modern artist.

While recognizing that he was walking in the quicksands of aesthetic theory, Wiener's comments provide one kind of interpretation of some of the relations between art and science, which may or may not be true, and which certainly are not provable in the ordinary sense. But we can accept as true, I believe, the ample testimony that scientists and artists have a base of shared experience in their mutual "sense of wonder in nature, of freedom within her boundaries, and of unity with her in knowledge."

The relationship between technology and art is, in many respects, more direct and therefore more observable. New materials, new processes, new techniques, especially in the use of light, film, and of electronics, have all widened the boundaries of art and ushered in an era of multi-media artistic endeavor. Changing technology stimulates also experiments in point of view as well as innovation in substance and form. And this is not new.

August Heckscher is fond of telling that "the great art critic Berenson described in his letters how a single technological creation could overturn all the accepted patterns of art. Berenson said that early in the century, he had gone out to look at one of the Wright Brothers' early airplanes. He went on to say: "I cannot tell you how I hate this innocent monster which is going to destroy the world I love. It will destroy the world I love, the world of level vision or vision from down upwards, in other words, the whole way of looking at things that the artist had been taught to expect, all the rules of perspective, the sense of looking at solid objects from one fixed place on the earth. All that," said Berenson, "was being thrown out by the invention of the airplane."

The rapid pace of change, accelerated by the progress of science and technology, bears on the artist with an especially heavy impact. Heckscher says of Berenson's remarks on the impact of the airplane on the artist's view of the world that

the artist living in this changing world, if he is going to produce great art, is going to have to do one of two things, and both of these are helped or supported by his being part of the traditional environment of learning in our society. In the first place, the artist will have to borrow from the visions of those men who are themselves expanding the horizons of truth, from the physicists who are giving us a new sense of what material is . . . to the psychologists who are looking deeper into the human consciousness than men have ever looked before. In this environment, the artist attains some of the vision and some of the understanding that our confused society cannot always give him. . . . The university, with its sense of true seeking, being out on the furthest limits of knowledge, will give the artist some sense of the world which he must try to interpret. . . .

Some time ago I was rereading a favorite book, *As I Remember Him,* by the late Hans Zinsser. Zinsser was a first-rate scientist and physician and in the highest sense a humanist and occasionally a poet. And in this book he had some very wise things to say about the importance of the artist—visual, literary, or performing—to the world of science. He argued that the insights of the artist, and the re-enthronement of art in our life, can serve as vital guides and guardians of the objectives of progress. In his argument for art, he quoted Santayana's observation that there is a "high breathlessness about beauty that cancels lust and superstitions." Might art not also, asked Zinsser, "cancel materialism gone wild as well?" And might it not—"If it could move arm-in-arm with science—give direction and harmonious dignity to the new powers . . . that science provides?" And by enriching man's feelings, may it not help him avoid a sterile intellectualism? Certainly art and artists can increase the "qualitative richness and emotional range" which can be beneficial to the work of the scientist in seeking to enlarge our understanding.

These scattered observations about the many intersections between the arts and humanities and the sciences and engineering bring me finally to the culminating argument I wish to present: our society urgently needs more humanists and scientists as activists jointly working in the public arena on real-life problems. There are a multitude of public policy issues where there is urgent need in the national decision-making process for the diverse judgments and insights of humanists, scientists, engineers, and social scientists. Let me select just two, because I have recently been involved in both.

The first is the security of the United States as it is affected by nuclear weapons. We are in the midst of an intense national debate about the deployment of an anti-ballistic missile system. In order to deal wisely with such a question, it is important to penetrate an array of arcane complexities, many of them nontechnical, and to give the ABM its proper place in the total context of our national security. It is urgently important to invent new ways of making decisions about weapons systems that will command public confidence and insure wiser policies. So far we have not done this well, as the current ABM controversy reveals.

Recently, in testifying before a Senate committee on this matter, I made some suggestions about how our Government might better deal with such grave and fateful decisions about our nuclear strategic forces and policies. I proposed that the government, from time to time, should convene an *ad hoc* or blue ribbon committee of wise men from varied backgrounds to make an independent, comprehensive study in depth of our strategic forces and policies.

The commission that I have in mind should be made up not only of such experts as those drawn from the military, from science and technology, and from foreign affairs, but also of those who are accustomed to weighing great issues in terms of man's highest social responsibilities.

The task force should be independent of the Department of Defense and other government agencies which have a direct responsibility for formulating, advocating, and carrying out strategic programs. In its studies it should seek to gain an understanding of the relationships of all of our weapons systems and of the strategic options confronting this country in the years immediately ahead.

I do not propose that the findings of such a commission should necessarily carry more weight than studies conducted within government. I have great respect for the thoroughness and rigor which the government can bring to the formulation of policy decisions although it does not always do so. Independent studies, such as I suggest, might well serve to sharpen the government's own analyses. The task force's recommendations should be critically examined by the normal procedures of the government and considered in relation to proposals which have come from within government. Their special value would be that they would be *independent* conclusions reached by a group of competent citizens who were free of organizational loyalties, and who bring to bear a wide spectrum of insights and sensitivities, and who could, therefore, formulate their evaluations and recommendations without being constrained by any departmental or disciplinary commitments or biases. So often the roles and missions interests of the armed services influence and narrow defense decisions more than they should, and the task force I suggest could transcend these service interests. By virtue of its freedom from any vested interests, such a commission could also provide some reassurance to the growing number of citizens who are concerned about the "military-industrial complex" and its alleged influence on our strategic policies and programs.

In 1954, I chaired a large-scale study partaking of some of these characteristics, which was undertaken at the request of President Eisenhower, and I think it fair to say that the intensive and comprehensive study which resulted helped in reaching priority judgments about our weapons technology and related matters, and was ultimately viewed as helpful by the government agencies involved. This task fore, incidentally, included not only scientists and engineers but a gifted historian and representatives of other disciplines.

In playing its fundamental role in reaching decisions about these weapons systems, which require vast expenditures and which might have a fateful effect on our survival, Congress, I respectfully suggest, can benefit from independent assessments arising out of a variety of different outlooks and experiences. Essential as it is, I am not sure that

the conventional hearing is by itself sufficient to
provide Congress with the searching studies it
needs to cope with the complexities of great security issues such as that presented by the ABM. Is
it not possible that Congress, too, could benefit
from creating a variety of special task forces to
make studies in depth for its cognizant committees? It has been heartening to note the growing
practice of some Congressional committees to con-
tract for special studies and to engage consultants
who can do more than simply appear for brief
testimony. The public would also benefit if independent studies marked by thoroughness and
objectivity could be made available. It would be of
advantage if these studies were financed by private
funds. There are a growing number of scholars
in our universities who are engaged in interdisciplinary studies of public policy issues, including defense, and they constitute a growing pool
that can be tapped. I believe we could have modu-
lated some of the current cacophony and disagree-
ment about the ABM if we had mobilized the kind
of interdisciplinary systems study I advocate.

Some years back, Dr. James B. Conant made a
proposal that I do not believe has ever been tried
in a formal way. He advocated that in the con-
sideration of weapons of technical complexity and
great cost, there be a quasi-judicial review of proposals, including a form of adversary proceeding.
"When a question comes up to be settled," he

said, "one or more referees might hear the arguments pro and con. If there were no contrary arguments, some technical expert should be appointed to speak on behalf of the taxpayer against the proposed research and development. Then adequate briefs of the two or more sides should be prepared (not a compromise committee report.)" Conant went on to emphasize that today every citizen is a "party to an enormous new enterprise. His government has gone into the research and development business on a scale totally different from anything seen in the past. . . . Consequences of tremendous significance in terms of survival may hang on the way this work is carried on," and "the waste of enormous sums of money could threaten the soundness of our economy."

It is important for the policymaker and the public to have the benefit of listening to contending points of view on complex technical and strategic proposals such as the ABM, and also for them to recognize that many questions involving technical, policy, and humane issues cannot be answered with positive yes or no certainty. There are many such questions to which scientists or other specialists of equivalent competence, objectivity, and complete integrity will respond differently. I cannot fault either those who sincerely and thoughtfully favor an ABM deployment, or those who oppose, and both should have full opportunities to be heard.

The second and wholly different area of public policy where engineers and humanists together face a common challenge is in the improvement of television. In fact, the quality of television depends upon joint action by engineers and humanists, else in any truly humane sense the medium can fail. Senator Pastore's recent hearings on the possibly harmful social effects of current commercial television programs were symptomatic of a deep concern in our country that the miraculous and powerful technology of television has not been put to the best uses of American society.

Two years ago the Carnegie Commission on Educational Television declared in its report that a well-financed and well-directed educational television system substantially larger and far more pervasive and effective than that which now exists in the United States must be brought into being if the full needs of the American public are to be served. It advanced the concept of Public Television as that kind of programming which includes all that is of human interest and importance which is not appropriate or available for support by advertising and which is not arranged for formal instruction. Said the Carnegie Commission:

We have become aware of television as a technology of immense power, growing steadily more powerful. What confronts our society is the obligation to bring that technology into the full service of man, so that its power to move image and sound is consistently coupled with a power to move mind and spirit. Television should enable us not only to see and hear more vividly, but to understand more deeply.

So far, television of all kinds has largely failed to provide this kind of service.

Since the Carnegie Commission report appeared, Congress has acted upon its principal recommendations and passed the Public Broadcasting Act, designed to build a noncommercial television system which can provide a much needed supplement to commercial television. This Act called for the establishment of the Corporation for Public Broadcasting, and this is now in being under strong leadership, although the funds yet made available are very small. With this landmark legislation, the American people have available to them a plan and an instrument which, if their potentials are realized, can offer the artist, the technician, the journalist, the scholar, the scientist, and the humanist a new freedom to create, innovate, and be heard.

In a letter to the Carnegie Commission, Mr. E. B. White summed up the potential of noncommercial or 'public' television when he said:

Noncommercial television should address itself to the ideal of excellence, not the idea of acceptability—which is what keeps commercial television from climbing the staircase. I think television should be the visual counterpart of the literary essay, should arouse our dreams, satisfy our hunger for beauty, take us on journeys, enable us to participate in events, present great drama and music, explore the sea and the sky and the woods and the hills. It should be our Lyceum, our Chautauqua, our Minsky's, and our Camelot. It should restate and clarify the social dilemma and the political pickle. Once in a while it does, and you get a quick glimpse of its potential.

Educational television also has had its great failure. It has not yet come close to mastering television technology for instructional purposes. This technology is advancing rapidly. Perhaps one of the most revolutionary of all developments is the impending technology of low-cost storage and playback of television programs—the possibility that in the future both black and white and color television programs can be purchased in the form of cassettes or records which can be inserted into an instrument plugged into the television set and played at will. The impact of this technology can be very great in multiplying the choices available to the home and the school and in making it possible to utilize program materials in much the same way that one plays phonograph records and, thus, break away from the fixed schedule.

The second impending major change in communications technology is the use of the communications satellite. In facilitating and multiplying the transmission of programs, communication satellites pose great issues of public policy. How should they be financed and managed? And should or should they not be used to bring a high degree of centralization in programming, both for the home and for the school? The communications satellite may well make it possible to broadcast from a central point directly into the school and home, thus leapfrogging over the local station or the state system and threatening a new kind of national regimentation and conformity. This is a problem of tremendous moment, and it will require the combined wisdom of the humanist and technologist to arrive at the best answer.

Next, there are immense possibilities ahead for extending television technology into wholly new domains. I speak of such concepts as interactive television, which would permit the viewer to communicate with the performer. I speak of arrangements to multiply the number of program choices available; of the concept of "narrowcasting" for reaching the small, select audience, or the many different, small, select audiences.

In commenting upon these technological possibilities, a consultant to the Carnegie Commission, Dr. J. C. L. Licklider, who is a psychologist and communications engineer, and educator, made this observation:

The main trend of educational television is somewhat too conservative in its estimation of the feasibility of selective, interactive, and intercommunicational television systems and of the achievability, with the aid of such systems, of a significant breakthrough in education. The main factor that is not sufficiently appreciated, I believe, is the effectiveness of interactive participation in a well-designed, strongly reinforcing educational process. Advances in technology are making it possible for the first time to set up such a process without depending upon lavish use of scarce human resources. Other advances are making it at least conceivable that we may be able to set up such processes on a broad enough scale to reach almost every educable member of the society. My conclusion, therefore, is that the situation calls for intensive research in two complementary fields: the exploitability of informational technology in support of education, and education within the new context offered by informational technology.

One does not need to embrace the metaphysics of Marshall McLuhan to see the enormous responsibilities which rest upon both the engineers and the humanists, the generalists and the politicians and all people who are concerned about the public welfare to salvage television technology to serve the best man and not the worst. I can think of no better example of the need for humanists, artists, and engineers to join forces to enhance the quality of our society.

Let me conclude by reporting on what I see to be the growing role of the humanities in those institutions such as Auburn in which science and technology are fully embraced. In such a setting, humanists have an opportunity to pursue liberal teaching and liberal learning in an atmosphere of exceptional freedom to innovate and to extend the scope of the humanities and to teach them in fresh ways that have a renewed relevance to contemporary affairs. They have, therefore, an opportunity also to advance the humanities in new ways, but in the great tradition of humane learning and without any sense of being either subordinate or superior to science. I do not propose a kind of scientific humanism, nor do I suggest we develop the humanities in the image of science. I believe, as Jacob Bronowski, that "every cast of mind has its creative activity which explores the likeness appropriate to it. . . ." The humanities as humanities have an opportunity to flourish in this environment just as the social sciences have.

But there is another aspect of the study of man that is of growing importance in institutions such as Auburn and my own, where science and engineering have important emphasis. In these institutions, with their great strength in science and engineering, the humanist, the social scientist, the engineer, the scientist, the planner, the artist, and the architect can form—and are forming—unique coalitions of resources to serve man and society.

We are currently examining at my own institution a program or center for policy studies with the thought that it might provide a new way for the university to involve itself constructively in

current public issues and in the process educate a
new kind of professional man who can bring a
systems approach to socio-technical matters and
who has the breadth to formulate policies and ac-
tions which are beyond the scope of the specialist.
Such a program of policy studies, if it is to be
effective, must include the arts and humanities as
well as science, engineering, and social studies.
The humanists, who have so far not been so ready
as the engineers to involve themselves in systems
studies, have a special opportunity to put the humanities to work through participation in such
policy studies concerned with the real and urgent
problems of contemporary society.

Even though they may be predominantly science or engineering, these collective efforts demonstrate humanism in action directed to goals
highly relevant to the urgent needs of a technological society. These socio-technical or scientific-hu-
manistic programs include such undertakings as
programs in urban affairs, in bioengineering and
living systems, in health-related activities, in
psycho-social studies of man-machine relationships,
and in the pursuit of the life sciences. In all these
programs there is a preoccupation with specific
problems relating to the human condition, such as
poverty and pollution, urban reconstruction, better
housing, better transportation, a benign environment. There is gathering determination to counter
the effects of harmful technological fall-out and,

more positively, to anticipate and avoid such fall-out in the future. There is a widening effort to identify and mobilize the powers inherent in science and engineering qualitatively to enrich our society.

If our technological society is to be made to work and be humane, if we are to make headway in solving the horrendous problems which confront us, there must be a continuing emphasis on these collective efforts to invent new ways, new programs, and new organizational arrangements whereby science and engineering, the arts, the social sciences, and the humanities work in partnership and bring their resources sensitively to bear on the contemporary needs of our society.

What I describe, then, is a kind of institution in which a constellation of collective efforts are invested with humanistic purpose. Each of the great disciplines, whether they be science, social science, humanities, or the arts, pursuing their teaching and research according to their own ways and traditions, come together in the fellowship of one great humanistic enterprise.

These lectures are but another manifestation of this interweaving and interdependence of these great fields in seeking to meet the relevant and urgent needs of man in a technological society and to construct a new and unified vision of the full potential of man. Walter Pater aptly stated the goal; "Here artists and philosophers and those whom the action of the world has elevated and made keen, do not live in isolation but breathe a common air, and catch light and heat from each other's thoughts."

APRIL, 1969

"You're *already* on board a spaceship—
Earth...and there are an infinite number of
resources out there and we'll never run out.
And there's an infinite amount of space in
which you can get rid of all your filth...."

—R. Buckminster Fuller

In the recent floodtide of doomful prophecies about
the imminent destruction of our environment, this
book stands virtually alone.

The three eminent scientists who wrote it offer hope
—and, more than that: positive, creative ideas that
can enable man to improve life on this planet and
build what Dr. James Killian, Jr., calls "the benign
environment." They point the way to a revolution in
approaching our problems—and suggest a new kind
of man, whom Dr. Fuller calls a "comprehensivist"
—a broad-gauged creator who can truly harness all
the fantastic tools of this new age on "Spaceship
Earth."

For, as Buckminster Fuller says in this book: "Man
is quite clearly like the hydrogen atom...designed
to be a success. He is a fantastic piece of design."

R. Buckminster Fuller's unique accomplishments as scientist,
philosopher, mathematician, and writer have made him one of
the most admired of Americans. He is popularly best known for
his invention of the geodesic dome.

James R. Killian, past President and currently Chairman of the
Corporation of Massachusetts Institute of Technology, was
special assistant for science and technology to President
Eisenhower and chairman of President Kennedy's Foreign
Intelligence Advisory Board.

Eric A. Walker, President of Pennsylvania State University, was
chief editor of the *Goals Report* of the American Society for
Engineering Education, a publication destined to have a strong
influence on the future direction of scientific education in the
United States.

COLLIER BOOKS
866 THIRD AVENUE, NEW YORK, N.Y. 10022